The New
PASSOVER
MENU

The New
PASSOVER
MENU

PAULA SHOYER

AUTHOR OF *THE HOLIDAY KOSHER BAKER*

STERLING EPICURE
New York

STERLING EPICURE

New York

An Imprint of Sterling Publishing
1166 Avenue of the Americas
New York, NY 10036

ISBN 978-1-4549-1440-2

Library of Congress Cataloging-in-Publication Data

Shoyer, Paula, author.
  The new Passover menu : a fresh look at Passover meals / Paula Shoyer, author of The holiday kosher baker.
    pages cm
  Summary: "Passover is a celebration of freedom—and Paula Shoyer's innovative Passover collection celebrates culinary
freedom, while still honoring the holiday's dietary rules. Her dishes will set you free, combining all the nostalgic pleasure of
family favorites with 65 contemporary creations sure to please a new generation of creative cooks. Covering both Seder
nights and all eight days of the holiday, Shoyer redefines Passover dining with an updated and global menu that includes
Banana Charoset, Peruvian Roast Chicken with Salsa Verde, Moroccan Spiced Short Ribs, Sweet Potato Tzimmes, Eggplant
Parmesan, and Frittata with Broccoli and Leeks. And don't forget the desserts (many gluten-free) that are Shoyer's
specialty, including Triple-Chocolate Biscotti, Opera Cake, and Pear Frangipane Tart. To streamline your planning, there
are eight full menus to use as is or to mix and match, along with suggestions for other meals. Passover has never been so
easy or delicious!"—Provided by publisher.
  Includes bibliographical references and index.
  ISBN 978-1-4549-1440-2 (hardback)
  1. Passover cooking. I. Title.
  TX739.2.P37S56 2015
  641.5676437--dc23
                                        2014037153

Distributed in Canada by Sterling Publishing
c/o Canadian Manda Group, 664 Annette Street
Toronto, Ontario, Canada M68 2CB
Distributed in the United Kingdom by GMC Distribution Services
Castle Place, 166 High Street, Lewes, East Sussex, England BN7 1XU
Distributed in Australia by Capricorn Link (Australia) Pty. Ltd.
P.O. Box 704, Windsor, NSW 2756, Australia

For information about custom editions, special sales, and premium and corporate purchases,
please contact Sterling Special Sales at 800-805-5489 or specialsales@sterlingpublishing.com.

Manufactured in Canada

2 4 6 8 10 9 7 5 3 1

www.sterlingpublishing.com

Photographs by Michael Bennett Kress

For all the kosher baker fans who asked me
to write a cookbook of savory recipes.
But, as my friend Suzin Glickman believes,
you should still eat dessert first.

CONTENTS

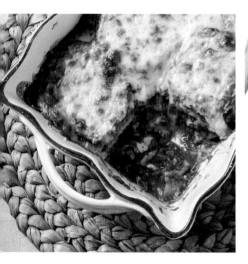

FREEDOM FROM PASSOVER FOOD OPPRESSION

P assover celebrates the Exodus of the Israelites from Egyptian slavery and features the universal theme of triumph over oppression. Elie Wiesel calls Passover "the "story of hope." During the holiday, we retell the story, perform rituals, and eat foods to reenact the experience of the Israelites. Jews who host the holiday often feel that preparing the house and food for Passover makes them feel a little too much like the Israelite slaves. *The New Passover Menu* has arrived in order to set you free.

Passover is the central Jewish holiday for entertaining, and families get together for all or part of the eight-day holiday. Passover food evokes many different memories and emotions. Some people recall delicious meals in their mothers' or grandmothers' homes and recipes that have been passed down through the generations. Others will roll their eyes and lament heavy kugels, dry desserts, and the weight of a holiday that brings many restrictions.

During Passover, Jewish people have to cook and bake within very stringent food restrictions that include no bread, rice, corn, oats, rye, spelt, barley, legumes, and pasta—and most people live in areas where there are no kosher-for-Passover restaurants or bakeries. Over the centuries, rabbis have expanded the prohibition against leavened bread to include any food that contains the prohibited ingredients, or which has come in direct contact with them. These foods are considered *chametz* and are forbidden during the holiday. It is the custom of Sephardic Jews to eat rice and legumes during Passover.

I wanted to write this book because, whenever I travel or tour the world as a kosher baker and cookbook author, people ask me about Passover food and desserts, no matter what time of year it is. Cooking for Passover meals weighs on people. I have always viewed the holiday's dietary restrictions as challenges that can be overcome, if you focus on the ingredients that you *can* use.

The New Passover Menu features updated traditional dishes that provide the nostalgic pleasure of family favorites, along with a raft of contemporary recipes developed to please creative cooks who do not want to compromise their taste for sophisticated recipes during the holiday. Armed with this book and the bonanza of Passover ingredients that are available today, you can enjoy delicious, elegant, and inspired holiday meals—and create new Passover food memories at the same time.

Paula

HOW TO USE THIS BOOK

To streamline your holiday planning, I've divided the book into eight menus: There are two Seder menus, one menu each for Shabbat and Yom Tov, and four diverse weekday menus. In addition, there is a chapter on breakfast foods and one on desserts that includes fifteen new recipes, most of which are gluten-free. You can follow the menus as they are, or mix and match them as you like. I've also included an equipment list for each recipe, so you'll know which tools you will need, along with preparation and cooking times, and tips to help with meal planning and storage. As I have not accounted for every meal during the eight-day holiday, here are menu suggestions for lunches and other meals:

WEEKDAY LUNCH MENUS

Frittata with Broccoli and Leeks (page 84)
Spinach with Apples and Raisins (page 47)

Sephardic Poached Fish in Pepper Sauce (page 18)
Gratin Dauphinois (page 53)
Roasted Asparagus with Toasted Almond and Orange Gremolata (page 34)

Seder Plate Salad (page 32)
Roasted Eggplant with Bell Pepper Vinaigrette (page 72)

Potato Gnocchi with Pink Sauce (page 64)
Broccoli with Garlic (page 11)
Beet and Butternut Squash Salad (page 41)
Eggplant Parmesan (page 63)

ITALIAN VEGETARIAN MENU (page 59)

FRENCH DAIRY MENU (page 51)

SHABBAT OR HOLIDAY LUNCH MENUS

Coconut Schnitzel with Almond Butter Sauce (page 44)
Garlic and Rosemary Mashed Potatoes (page 33)
Roasted Peppered Carrots (page 77)
Brussels Sprouts and Shallots (page 24)

Zucchini Basil Soup (page 38)
Moroccan Spiced Short Ribs (page 22)
Cauliflower Slabs with Basil Pesto (page 46)
Roasted Vegetables with Tarragon (page 24)

Gingered Red Pepper and Tomato Soup (page 17)
Peruvian Roasted Chicken with Salsa Verde (page 8)
Crunchy Quinoa with Sweet Potatoes and Cranberries (page 78)
Mixed Vegetable Antipasti (page 60)

Caramelized Onion and Sweet Potato Soup (page 28)
Whole Chicken with Dried Fruit Stuffing (page 21)
Garlic and Rosemary Mashed Potatoes (page 33)
Asparagus, Zucchini, and Leek Kugel (page 13)

Sephardic Poached Fish in Pepper Sauce (page 18)
Kale Caesar Salad (page 52)
Gratin Dauphinois (page 53)
Brussels Sprouts and Shallots (page 24)

THE PASSOVER PANTRY

All processed food consumed during Passover must have the "Kosher for Passover" designation. There are exceptions, but the list changes from year to year, so you should always check the newest guidelines. All the ingredients I use in this book are available with Passover certification, though you may not find everything where you live. New products hit the market every year, and you can find many Passover ingredients online.

KITNIYOT

The term *kitniyot* refers to certain grains, legumes, and seeds that are not expressly forbidden on Passover but that Ashkenazic Jews do not eat during the holiday. Examples include rice and corn, lentils, beans, peas, peanuts, and soybeans, and such seeds as amaranth, mustard, sesame, poppy, fennel, cardamom, and sunflower. Ashkenazic Jews do not use these ingredients during Passover for two reasons: The first is that some of them can be made into food that looks like *chametz*. The second is that many of these items are typically stored in sacks used for the five prohibited grains: wheat, barley, rye, oats, and spelt. My family tradition is to refrain from eating *kitniyot*, so these ingredients are not included in this book.

GEBROKTS

Some Jews follow a custom of not eating *gebrokts*, the Yiddish word for any matzoh, or matzoh product, mixed with liquid, because of the chance that the liquid might cause any unbaked flour in the matzoh to become *chametz*. I have noted any recipes that are *gebrokts*.

PASSOVER COOKING AND BAKING SUBSTITUTES

- 1 cup flour = ¾ cup (120g) potato starch plus ¼ cup (35g) matzoh cake meal

- 1 tablespoon flour = ½ tablespoon potato starch

- 1 tablespoon cornstarch = 1 tablespoon potato starch

- 1 cup confectioners' sugar = 1 cup minus 1 tablespoon (190g) granulated sugar plus 1 tablespoon potato starch pulsed in a food processor or blender until it becomes a very fine powder

- ½ cup corn syrup = ⅔ cup (130g) granulated sugar plus ½ cup (120ml) water boiled for 2 to 3 minutes or until it starts to thicken; let cool and then store in a jar or container. (May also use equivalent amounts of honey as a corn syrup substitute.)

- 1 cup vanilla sugar = 1 cup (200g) granulated sugar plus 1 split vanilla bean left to sit for 24 hours in a tightly covered jar

- 1 teaspoon cream of tartar = 1½ teaspoons lemon juice or 1½ teaspoons white vinegar

PREPARING FOR PASSOVER

In addition to the prohibition against eating *chametz*—any leavened food or food that has come in contact with leavened products—there are rules that apply to utensils and cooking and baking equipment as well. Anything you use during the rest of the year that comes in contact with *chametz* may not be used during Passover, unless it is made of a material that may be *kashered* and is thoroughly cleaned and heated to purge any *chametz* it may have absorbed.

However difficult a mind game it may be to play, I like to look at Passover cleaning as an opportunity to thoroughly clean every part of my kitchen. All of us should go through our kitchen drawers and cabinets and remove crumbs on a regular basis. But let's admit it—who does? So, every year, Passover gives us an a chance to purge our pantries of ingredients that have long expired, or that have been used only once, and donate food that we'll never use. Wipe those shelves clean!

Many people maintain separate dishes and utensils for Passover, but some things may be *kashered* (made kosher) for Passover. You are permitted to *kasher* stainless steel pans if the pan is made from one piece of metal and has no crevices, but you cannot *kasher* anything made of plastic, china, pottery, or ceramic. Whether or not you can *kasher* glass is an issue that rabbis debate. Some say that all it needs is a good cleaning to be used on Passover, while others hold that you cannot *kasher* it at all. You should consult your rabbi regarding a ruling on glass. Any items that are impossible to completely clean, such as strainers, graters, and food processor blades, may not be *kashered* either.

All major kitchen appliances and your stovetop must be thoroughly cleaned and scrubbed, and then *kashered*. Small appliances, sinks, and kitchen surfaces must also be scrubbed and *kashered*. The refrigerator should be cleaned and the shelves lined with paper towels, waxed paper, or something similar. Check with your rabbinic authority for specific guidance regarding these and all Passover preparation rules.

SELLING *CHAMETZ*

Jews are forbidden to have any *chametz* in their possession, so it must be sold to a non-Jew before the holiday. Today you can do this through your synagogue or online.

SEARCHING FOR *CHAMETZ* AND BURNING IT

In my family, on the night before Passover, we walk around the house and search for any remaining *chametz*. We place ten pieces of bread around the house and walk from room to room with a lit candle and a paper bag. We use a long feather to push the bread into the bag. The next day we burn the collected *chametz*. I can still remember the strange looks from the neighbors, as my father, Reubin Marcus, made a small fire at the street curb every year when I was growing up and tossed the remaining bread into the fire. This ritual was pretty exciting for a small child who had never gone camping.

THE SEDER

The Passover Seder is the most widely celebrated Jewish ceremony in the Jewish calendar, even by Jews who are not otherwise observant of Jewish holidays. It is a joyous evening full of wine, good food, and song. On the same night, all over the world, Jewish families are reading the same words and discussing the same ideas, no matter what language they speak.

According to food historian Gil Marks, the Seder evolved over time, and Jews under Roman rule adopted many of the dining rituals of the day, including hand-washing and reclining. In addition, we eat eggs before the meal, which goes back to a Greco-Roman tradition.

At the Seder (a Hebrew word for "order"), we read the Haggadah (retelling), which relates the story of the Israelite Exodus from Egypt, perform certain rituals, and eat a festive meal. The Torah commands us to teach this story to our children, and discussion is encouraged. The Haggadah states that every Jew must regard himself or herself as if he or she was personally freed from Egypt. In my family we accomplish this by discussing contemporary forms of slavery.

MY PASSOVER SEDERS

The Seder of my childhood was hosted by my father, Reubin Marcus, and was very by the book. On rare occasions, my father allowed his day school–educated children to share what they learned, but only as long as it did not interfere with the recitation of every single word of the Haggadah. My mother invited relatives, and the food was good. We all sang the songs off-key with different tunes, but that added some comedy. I was always left with the feeling that there could have been more discussion—or *something* to vary the experience from year to year.

As a junior in college, I spent a semester at The Hebrew University of Jerusalem. That year, I joined my Israel-born roommate, Limor Decter, and her grandparents, countless aunts, uncles, and cousins for Passover. In Israel, Jews only celebrate one Seder, so we divided our time between the Kivitys, her mother's Iraqi family in Ramat Gan, and the Cohens, her father's Moroccan family in Bnei Brak.

We went to the Iraqis first and stayed all the way through a delicious meal. Then we walked the mile plus to the Moroccans, where we ate another entire meal (this one with rice!) and stayed until about two A.M.—the four cups of wine and the Haggadah songs were just a starting point for Limor's uncles. We American college students had never experienced a Seder that was a true party— we sang and drank for hours. It opened up my eyes to the possibility of Seders being truly fun.

When I married my husband, Andy, I was told that the Rosenberg family Seder, on his father's side, was a really big deal. Over forty people gathered in a rented space for a catered meal, with the Seder led by Andy's father, Arthur Shoyer, may his memory be a blessing. The problem for me was that the food was not kosher, so I had to bring my own. Over the years, that became burdensome as our family grew to six. We ate our food cold, while all the cousins had hot matzoh ball soup, something that did not always elicit smiles from my then-young children.

My kids adapted, as the Seder was joyous and full of cousins they saw only once a year. In addition, everyone in Andy's family has a truly spectacular voice, so the singing was special and they sang lovely family tunes from Romania. Yet I was disappointed that the Seder was quite abridged: The first part, consisting of the retelling of the Exodus story, was brief, and focused on the highlights, after which we proceeded to the meal. The second half of the Seder consisted solely of the major songs, leaving grace after meals, the Hallel section, and minor songs untouched.

At some point, Andy and I decided that there had to be something better than a Seder where you just read all the words, and one where you skipped half of them. So we started hosting our own Seders. Andy leads the Seder surrounded by a pile of Haggadahs and commentaries and shares readings from them. A major part of our Seder is the Exodus story told in the form of a play written by Andy. One year a guest, Kayla Drogosz, brought a bag of costumes, and the teens at the table dressed as Pharaoh, Moses, and Israelite women.

We incorporate both Andy's Romanian tunes and those from my childhood. Our children share insights they learned in school, and we talk about our own struggles and how we can overcome them as the Israelites did theirs. Our favorite tradition takes place during the song "Chad Gadya"—everyone gets to be a character from the song and has to develop a sound to represent it. We go around the table and each person makes the sound on cue. We love to hear the grandfathers make sounds like a dog or goat, and somehow there's always someone who can create hilarious sounds for fire and water. Everyone at the table laughs and laughs.

My family spent Passover 2013 in Israel and had the Seder at my brother Ezra Marcus's house in Kadima. Because there were relatives from the United States and Brazil in attendance, every line was translated into English and Portuguese. The delicious food was catered from a local kosher kibbutz. I look forward to the Seders of my future.

FROGS

During the Seder we recite the ten plagues that G-d unleashed on the Egyptian people when Pharaoh repeatedly refused to let the Israelites leave Egypt. Because of the plagues, frogs have become one of the symbols children can identify with during the Seder. When my children were young, they had "Plagues in a Bag," little stuffed items to play with during the Seder that represented each of the plagues. One year we gave the children tiny plastic frogs that they threw around while we recited the plagues. For those fearful of tiny plastic frogs landing in bowls of salt water, this might not be the way to go.

My best frog story goes back to October 2013, when I was teaching a baking class hosted by the Jewish Community Center and Chabad of Hong Kong. I was invited to a delicious Shabbat dinner at the home of Nealy and Seth Fischer. Seth told me that, one Passover in Hong Kong, he went down to the reptile market in Kowloon and bought live frogs. At the appointed time, he released them at the table, and the kids were delighted. How do you top that?

THE PASSOVER TABLE

As is the case with all Shabbat and holiday meals, Jewish hosts endeavor to create beautiful tables. Many of us grew up with our mothers' starched white linen tablecloths and simple china, and now want a different look to complement our modern menus. I have provided some suggestions for table settings throughout this book. Make sure to have some short vases on hand, as tall ones obscure views and hinder conversation. I learned from master entertainer Elena Lefkowitz to layer multiple cloths and even arrange placemats on top of tablecloths to make your table more interesting. Place cards save time.

and falls within the category of vegetables for which you recite the prayer *"borei p'ri ha'adamah"* during the Seder.

MAROR AND CHAZERET: These bitter herbs represent the bitterness of slavery. You can use romaine lettuce or white horseradish (jarred or freshly grated).

CHAROSET: Charoset is a paste that looks like the mortar that the slaves used to build bricks. It is made from apples, nuts, and sometimes dried fruit; for recipes, see pages 2 and 16.

ZEROA: The roasted shank bone recalls the paschal lamb eaten on the night of the Exodus and the Passover offering in the Temple. Roast a chicken or other meat bone in the oven until browned.

BEITZA: The roasted egg represents the sacrifices made in the Temple. To prepare it, boil an egg and then roast it by holding it over the flame on your stovetop.

In a new tradition, some people also place an orange on the Seder plate to commemorate the role of women in Jewish life.

MATZOH

Matzoh is the iconic Passover food. We eat matzoh because, when the Israelites were departing Egypt in haste, there was no time for their bread to rise. The word *matzoh* comes from the word *moootz*, which means "to press."

During the Seder, the host breaks the middle of three matzohs in half, wraps one half, and then hides it. This is called the Afikoman, which means "dessert"; it is eaten at the end of the festive meal. Traditionally, children hide the Afikoman and at the end of the meal negotiate with the person leading the Seder for its return.

THE SEDER PLATE

Most families have one large Seder plate on the table. I learned from my husband's family to create individual plates with all the items that will be eaten and dipped during the Seder, as shown above. It saves time when passing them around to thirty people or more.

THE SEDER PLATE AND TABLE FOODS

The Seder plate is a visual retelling of the Passover story. There are different customs about what is placed on it. Here are the items placed on the Seder plate according to my family custom.

KARPAS: *Karpas* is a vegetable that represents spring and the flourishing of the Israelites when they first came down to Egypt. You can use parsley, celery, or potato, which was historically used when other vegetables were not available

Matzoh is baked under close rabbinic supervision. No more than 18 minutes may pass from the time the flour is initially moistened with water until the matzoh comes out of the oven. If more time than that elapses, it will be *chametz.* When I was in elementary school, I went on a field trip with my classmates to a matzoh factory in Brooklyn. I remember how hot the little room was and that the religious men baking the matzohs kept chanting "Matzohs are the mitzvot of Hashem (G-d, in Hebrew)." Matzoh-baking was done by hand until 1838, when machines took over; in America, machine baking began in 1925.

Shmura matzohs are the large, some would say ugly, round matzohs that many people serve at Seders. Whether shmura matzoh is handmade or created by machine, every step in the preparation of it is done under much tighter supervision than regular matzoh—the wheat is guarded from the time it is harvested, when it is taken to be milled, and it is watched carefully throughout the baking process.

Regular matzoh has only two ingredients: flour and water. Egg matzohs contain eggs and are made with fruit juice instead of water. Within the Ashkenazic community, egg matzoh is not eaten on Passover except by children, the elderly, and people who are sick or infirm or who cannot digest regular matzoh.

SALT WATER
Bowls of salt water for dipping the *karpas* and egg recall the sweat and tears of the Israelites and the splitting of the Red Sea.

FOUR CUPS OF WINE
During the Seder, we consume four cups of wine. At the Seder, red wine is typically served. For most of my life that has meant the sticky, sweet,

kosher kind. Jewish families, including my own, now take advantage of the wonderful new world of kosher wines and drink high-quality wines at the Passover Seder. We drink wine because it symbolizes freedom, and the color of the wine recalls the blood that Jews placed on their doorposts during the last plague, the slaughter of the firstborn, in order to protect themselves.

Because of a debate among Talmud scholars about whether there should be a fifth cup of wine at the Seder, the rabbis added Elijah's cup, which is placed on the table but not consumed.

UPDATED ASHKENAZIC SEDER MENU

These are the recipes I serve to my own family for the Passover Seder. They reflect a connection to my Ashkenazic food traditions, along with a taste for modern and global flavors. Indeed, because many Jewish cooks search online and pore over their cookbook collections to prepare contemporary holiday menus, it is more important than ever that we endeavor to pass down the foods of our childhood to the next generation. I believe that some family recipes should be served every single year on holidays so that you give your children lasting food memories, but I suggest that you also find a way to contemporize part of the menu.

BANANA CHAROSET
{ gluten-free }

MAKES 3 CUPS (SERVES 25 FOR SEDER)
PREP TIME 10 minutes
ADVANCE PREP May be made 3 days in advance
EQUIPMENT Cutting board • Knives • Measuring cups and spoons • Food processor • Box grater • Silicone spatula • Small serving bowl

Charoset is the element on the Seder plate that represents the mortar used by the Israelite slaves to build bricks. Growing up, I had Seders almost exclusively at my parents' house or a handful of other relatives' homes, and everyone made the same charoset: walnuts, apples, and sweet wine all smooshed together. It was only when I began hosting my own Seders that I discovered a wide variety of charoset recipes from every corner of the world where Jews have ever resided. This recipe comes from my friend Melissa Arking, who is a fabulous cook. I added chopped walnuts at the end for some texture.

3 large ripe bananas
2 cups (240g) ground walnuts
2 tablespoons sugar
½ teaspoon ground cinnamon
2 tablespoons sweet kosher wine
2 apples, shredded on the large holes of a box grater
1 cup (120g) walnut halves, chopped into ⅓-inch (8-mm) pieces

IN THE BOWL of a food processor fitted with a metal blade, place the bananas, ground walnuts, sugar, cinnamon, and wine. Process until the mixture comes together. Transfer to a small bowl, add the apples and chopped walnuts, and stir to combine.

GROUND NUTS

You can buy nuts already ground, with the skin or without. I have a coffee grinder dedicated to grinding nuts. You can also use a food processor, as long as it can reduce the nuts to a fine grind, almost like a powder, when you need almond flour for baking. If you grind nuts for too long, you will end up with nut butter.

FRESH SALMON GEFILTE FISH LOAF WITH ARUGULA, AVOCADO, AND MANGO SLAW

SERVES 8

PREP TIME 2 hours to thaw fish, 10 minutes to assemble loaf, 15 minutes to make salad

COOK TIME 45 minutes

ADVANCE PREP Dressing and loaves may be made 2 days in advance; baked loaf needs to chill in fridge overnight.

EQUIPMENT 8-inch (20-cm) loaf pan • Parchment paper • Silicone spatula • Medium and large bowls • Small bowl • Cutting board • Knives • Garlic press • Measuring cups and spoons

Sometimes my Polish ancestors look kindly upon me, and my homemade gefilte fish emerges from the stock perfectly formed and tasting great. Other years, they taste flat. One year they disintegrated and I had an enormous pot of gefilte soup. Mindful of all the preparation that goes into hosting a Seder, I came up with this simple and beautiful alternative to schlepping to the fish market and smelling up the house. This recipe for fresh salmon encased in gefilte fish serves about eight people, but you can make as many loaves as you like. If you are using a disposable loaf pan for this recipe, bake the loaf for an additional 10 minutes.

FOR THE FISH LOAF

1 roll (22 ounce/625g) frozen gefilte fish loaf
2 teaspoons oil for greasing pan
13 ounces (370g) salmon fillet, skin removed

FOR THE SLAW

1/2 cup (120ml) mayonnaise
3 tablespoons (45ml) fresh orange juice (from 1 orange)
4 teaspoons honey
1 clove garlic, crushed
1/4 teaspoon ground ginger
1/2 red onion, finely chopped (about 1/2 cup/80g)
Salt and black pepper
1/2 head green cabbage, cut in half and thinly sliced (about 2 cups/140g)
5 ounces (140g) arugula leaves
3 scallions, thinly sliced
1 ripe mango, cut into 3/4-inch (2-cm) cubes
1/3 cup (45g) dried cranberries
1 avocado, cut into 3/4-inch (2-cm) cubes

~ continued ~

3

To make the fish
PLACE the frozen gefilte fish loaf in the fridge and let thaw overnight or let sit at room temperature for 2 hours until completely thawed.

PREHEAT oven to 325°F (160°C).

POUR 1 teaspoon of oil into the loaf pan and rub it all around the bottom and sides of the pan. Line with parchment paper, pressing it against the sides and into the corners. Add another teaspoon of oil and rub all around to coat the top and sides.

DIVIDE the thawed loaf between two bowls. Use a silicone spatula to break up the fish until it can be stirred. If your piece of salmon is thicker at one end than the other, trim off some of the top of the thicker end and place it on top of the thinner end. Spread half the gefilte fish into the bottom of the pan to cover. Place the fresh salmon on top, pressing it gently into the layer of gefilte fish. Use the spatula to scoop up and spread the remaining gefilte fish to cover the top and sides of the salmon.

COVER the pan tightly with aluminum foil and bake the fish loaf for 45 minutes. Let cool and then chill overnight in the fridge. When ready to serve, remove the foil and lift the parchment and loaf out of the pan and onto a cutting board. Cut into 1-inch-thick (2.5-cm) slices.

To make the slaw
IN A MEDIUM BOWL, whisk the mayonnaise, orange juice, honey, garlic, ginger, and red onion. Add salt and black pepper to taste.

IN A LARGE BOWL, combine the cabbage, arugula, scallions, mango, and cranberries. Add the dressing and toss. Just before serving, add the avocado. Serve the slaw next to the plated fish slices or in a separate bowl.

EGGS AND SALT WATER AND THE MARCUS FAMILY SOUP

At the beginning of the festive meal, we serve small bowls of salt water with a hard-boiled egg. My aunt Lillian Polansky, may her memory be a blessing, used to serve this cold soup:
Place about ¾ cup (180ml) of salted cold water per person into a large bowl. Peel and halve the hard-boiled eggs (one egg per person) and remove the yolks. In a small bowl, mash the yolks with a fork, add to the salt water, and mix well. Cut the whites into ½-inch (12-mm) pieces and add to the bowl. Trim and thinly slice four scallions for every six people and add to the bowl. Season the soup with black pepper to taste, stir, and serve cold.

BOILING EGGS

Place eggs in a saucepan with water to cover. Bring to a boil, reduce the heat to low, and simmer for 8 minutes. Pour off the boiling water and replace with cold water to stop the cooking. May be made 4 days in advance.

TRIMMING SCALLIONS

Cut off just a sliver of the scallion from the very end of the white base and another sliver from the green part. Peel the outer green layer down toward the white base and discard. Rinse well.

CHICKEN SOUP WITH CHICKEN MEATBALLS AND ZUCCHINI SPAGHETTI

SERVES 14–16
PREP TIME 25 minutes
COOK TIME 2 hours, 8 minutes
ADVANCE PREP Soup may be made 3 days in advance or frozen; meatballs may be made 1 day in advance
EQUIPMENT Measuring cups and spoons • Large soup pot • Cutting board • Knives • Vegetable peeler • 2 medium bowls • Large sieve or strainer • Garlic press • Food processor

Like most people, I love matzoh balls. Although everyone knows me as a from-scratch baker, I am admitting here that I always make matzoh balls from the mix. After eating my mother's matzoh balls for years, which alternated from year to year between light and fluffy and something else (I think because of variations in egg sizes), once I tried the balls from the mix, I never went back. Constant dieting has forced me to avoid them, so I developed chicken meatballs as an alternative. They even look like matzoh balls. But the traditionalists out there need not worry, as I have also provided ideas below for updating traditional matzoh balls.

FOR THE SOUP
2 whole medium chickens, cut into pieces
2 large onions, quartered
6 carrots, peeled and cut in half
1 leek, white and light green parts only, cut lengthwise in half
6 stalks celery with leaves, cut crosswise in half
4 cloves garlic, peeled
2 parsnips, peeled and cut in thirds
1 fennel bulb, quartered
1 turnip, peeled and quartered
2 bay leaves
1 tablespoon kosher salt
1 gallon (3.8L) water
½ bunch parsley (see box, page 30)
½ bunch dill (see box, page 30)
Salt and black pepper

FOR THE CHICKEN MEATBALLS
2 boneless chicken breasts (about 5–6 ounces each)
¼ cup (60ml) chicken stock
2 tablespoons ground almonds or matzoh meal
2 cloves garlic, crushed
1 large egg
2 scallions, thinly sliced
¼ teaspoon salt
¼ teaspoon black pepper

FOR THE GARNISH
2 medium zucchini, not peeled

To make the soup
PLACE the chicken pieces in a large pot. Add the onions, carrots, leek, celery, garlic, parsnips, fennel, turnip, bay leaves, and salt. Add the water and bring to a boil. Use a large spoon to skim the scum off the top of the soup. Cover the pot, reduce the heat to low, and let the soup simmer,

checking after 5 minutes and skimming off any additional scum. Add the parsley and dill, cover, and simmer for 2 hours. Let cool. Strain through a large sieve, reserving the carrots to return to the soup when serving. Taste the soup and add more salt or pepper if necessary.

To make the meatballs
WHILE the soup is cooking, prepare the meatball mixture. In the bowl of a food processor with the metal blade attachment, mix together the chicken, stock, ground almonds, garlic, and egg until a paste forms. Add the scallions, salt, and pepper and pulse a few times to mix. Transfer the meatball mixture to a medium bowl, cover with plastic wrap, and chill for up to 1 day, until ready to shape and cook the meatballs.

USE a spoon to scoop up the meatball batter and, with wet hands, shape it into 1½-inch (4-cm) balls. Bring the strained soup to a simmer, add the meatballs, cover, and cook for 8 minutes.

To make the garnish
MEANWHILE, prepare the zucchini "spaghetti" for the garnish. Slice the zucchini lengthwise into ¼-inch-thick (6mm) slices. Keeping the stack together, use a vegetable peeler to shave the zucchini into long strips. Slice the reserved cooked carrots into rounds and return them to the soup. Top each serving of soup and meatballs with some of the zucchini spaghetti.

MATZOH BALL VARIATIONS
{ gebrokts }

Combine your choice of any one of the following with one packet from a 5-ounce (142-g) package of matzoh ball mix to make 13 matzoh balls. Plan on 2 matzoh balls per person:

- 1 teaspoon fresh finely chopped ginger plus 2 teaspoons finely chopped cilantro leaves

- ½ teaspoon black pepper

- 1 carrot peeled and chopped into ¼-inch (6-mm) pieces

- 1½ teaspoons mixed finely chopped fresh herbs, such as rosemary, thyme, and basil (see box, page 30)

PERUVIAN ROASTED CHICKEN WITH SALSA VERDE

SERVES 4–6

PREP TIME 10 minutes for chicken, 30 minutes for sauce

COOK TIME 1 hour for chicken, 25 minutes for sauce

ADVANCE PREP Chicken may be made 1 day in advance; sauce may be made 1 week in advance

EQUIPMENT Cutting board • Knives • Measuring cups and spoons • Large roasting pan • Wooden spoon or silicone spatula • Medium frying pan • Food processor

For many years, our family has been blessed with Betty Supo, a wonderful do-it-all nanny. Among her many talents, she is a terrific cook and has introduced our family to flavorful Peruvian dishes. Her best is Arroz con Pollo with Salsa Verde (chicken with rice and a luscious green chili sauce). Here is the version that Betty and I cooked up so the world could enjoy a taste of Peru during Passover. If you like really spicy food, include the jalapeño pepper seeds in the frying pan along with the peppers.

FOR THE ROASTED CHICKEN

1 large whole chicken, cut into 8 pieces
4 teaspoons ground cumin
1 tablespoon paprika
2 teaspoons garlic powder
¼ teaspoon salt, plus more as needed
¼ teaspoon black pepper, plus more as needed
3 tablespoons extra virgin olive oil
1 head garlic, cloves separated, not peeled

FOR THE SALSA VERDE

2 tablespoons vegetable oil
4 cloves garlic, cut in half
1 medium onion, cut in half and sliced
2 jalapeño peppers, halved (remove seeds for a mild flavor; keep seeds for more heat)
Leaves from 1 large or 2 small bunches fresh cilantro
½ cup (120ml) water
½ teaspoon kosher salt

To make the chicken
PREHEAT oven to 400°F (200°C).

PLACE the chicken pieces in a large roasting pan. In a small bowl, combine the cumin, paprika, garlic powder, salt, and black pepper. Drizzle 1 tablespoon of the oil over the chicken and rub to coat. Shake the spice mixture onto the chicken and rub all over.

PLACE the garlic cloves in a small bowl and add the remaining 2 tablespoons (45ml) of oil. Season with salt and pepper and toss to coat. Scatter the garlic cloves and drizzle the oil over the chicken pieces. Bake, uncovered, for 50 minutes to 1 hour, or until well browned and the juices run clear.

To make the salsa verde
HEAT the oil in a medium frying pan over medium-high heat. Add the garlic and cook for 1 minute. Add the onions and cook for 3 to 5 minutes, or just until they soften. Add the jalapeño halves, open side down, and cook for 1 minute. Turn over and cook for another 4 minutes over medium-low heat, stirring occasionally, until the jalapeños are fork-tender.

LET COOL for 20 minutes. Place the jalapeño mixture in a food processor, add the cilantro leaves, water, and salt, and process until pureed and smooth. Cover and store in the fridge for up to 1 week. Serve the chicken on a platter and the salsa verde in a bowl alongside.

BRISKET
OSSO BUCO

SERVES 10

PREP TIME 15 minutes

COOK TIME 3 hours

ADVANCE PREP May be made 3 days in advance; add gremolata after brisket is reheated

EQUIPMENT Cutting board • Knives, including a good carving knife • Vegetable peeler • Measuring cups and spoons • Zester • Garlic press • Large frying pan with 2-inch (5-cm) sides or Dutch oven • Wooden spoon or silicone spatula • Small bowl

Osso buco is an Italian style of preparing veal shanks, round cuts of veal with a bone in the center. I first ate osso buco at Tevere 84, a kosher Italian restaurant in New York City, and I loved the fresh lemon and garlic gremolata, which is added at the end of the cooking time. The gremolata flavors give heavy, traditionally prepared brisket a springtime taste. I prefer to use second-cut brisket because it is more tender than first-cut brisket, which has too little fat.

FOR THE BRISKET

¼ cup (60ml) extra virgin olive oil

¼ cup (35g) matzoh cake meal or potato starch (40g)

1 (3-pound/1.4-kg) brisket

2 large onions, cut in half and sliced

2 carrots, peeled and thinly sliced into rounds

2 stalks celery, thinly sliced

1 bay leaf

½ cup (120ml) white wine

1 can (28 ounce/795g) whole peeled or diced tomatoes

2 tablespoons tomato paste, or ½ cup (120ml) tomato sauce

Salt and black pepper

FOR THE GREMOLATA

2 tablespoons finely chopped fresh parsley

4 cloves garlic, crushed

1 tablespoon lemon zest (from 1 lemon)

PREHEAT oven to 375°F (190°C).

HEAT the oil in a large frying pan with 2-inch (5-cm) sides or a Dutch oven over medium-high heat. Sprinkle the matzoh cake meal or potato starch on both sides of the meat, shaking off any excess, and brown both sides of the meat until crispy parts develop. Remove to a plate. Add the onions, carrots, celery, and bay leaf to the pan and cook over medium heat, using a wooden spoon or silicone spatula to scrape up any pieces of meat that are stuck to the bottom of the pan. Cook until the onions are translucent, about 5 minutes.

ADD the wine and cook until most of it has boiled off and only a little liquid is left around the vegetables. Add the canned tomatoes, including their juices, and tomato paste to the pan and bring to a boil. If you used a Dutch oven, return the meat to the pan. If you used a frying pan, transfer the vegetables and sauce to a baking pan and place the meat on top. Add salt and a generous amount of pepper. Cover tightly with aluminum foil and bake for 1½ hours.

MEANWHILE, prepare the gremolata. Combine the parsley, garlic, and lemon zest in a small bowl. Cover and place in the fridge until ready to serve. Gremolata may be made 1 day in advance.

REMOVE the pan from the oven, place the meat on a cutting board, and slice against the grain into ⅓-inch-thick (8-mm) slices. Return the slices to the pan, cover, and bake for another 1¼ hours. Sprinkle the gremolata over the meat in the pan, stirring some into the sauce.

BROWNING MEAT

During Passover, in the absence of flour, you can use either matzoh cake meal or potato starch to dredge meat or chicken before browning. Both flour substitutes work well, but the cake meal coating encourages better browning. To brown meat or chicken, place enough oil in a heavy pan over medium-high heat to cover the bottom. Add the dredged meat or chicken to the pan and cook until the pieces release from the pan on their own and have several crispy parts. Turn over and repeat.

BROCCOLI WITH GARLIC

SERVES 6–8
PREP TIME 5 minutes
COOK TIME 10 minutes
ADVANCE PREP May be made 2 days in advance
EQUIPMENT Cutting board • Knives • Measuring cups and spoons • Large saucepan • Colander • Silicone spatula • Garlic press

I prefer my vegetables either raw or just lightly cooked so they remain crisp. This Shoyer family staple is so good, it may just win over any child or adult who is not a big fan of broccoli. I use the blanching method from this recipe for cauliflower and string beans, as well (although not on Passover). Make sure not to overcook the broccoli.

9–10 cups (2.2–2.4L) water
1 teaspoon kosher salt
2 pounds (900g) broccoli, cut into 2-inch (5-cm) florets and pieces
2 tablespoons (30ml) extra virgin olive oil
3 cloves garlic, crushed
Salt and black pepper

IN A LARGE SAUCEPAN over high heat, bring the water and salt to a boil. Add the broccoli to the boiling water, return the water to a boil, and cook for 2 minutes, or just until you can slide a fork into the broccoli.

DRAIN immediately in a colander, and then run cold water over the broccoli until it stops steaming. Transfer the broccoli pieces to a clean dish towel or paper towels to dry and cool completely.

HEAT the oil in the same saucepan over medium heat. Add the garlic and cook for 1 minute. Add the broccoli and toss gently. Season with salt and pepper to taste. Serve immediately.

SWEET POTATO TZIMMES

SERVES 8
PREP TIME 15 minutes
COOK TIME 1½ hours
ADVANCE PREP May be made 3 days in advance
EQUIPMENT Cutting board • Knives • Vegetable peeler • Measuring cups and spoons • Large heavy saucepan • Silicone spatula • 9 x 13-inch (23 x 33-cm) baking pan

If you are from my generation, you might still know about the recipe box: a small box full of recipes written or printed on index cards. I received one at my bridal shower from my friends and relatives, who also gave me recipes cards that I still have in my box. Over the years I've stuffed the box with other cards people have given me, including this recipe, a tangy stew of sweet potato and dried fruit, with Debbie Snyder Kulp's name on it. I mentioned the recipe to Debbie a few years ago and she had no memory of it. My family has enjoyed it for years, however, and although I have made some changes, I am still giving Debbie credit. The cards do not lie.

2 cups (480ml) apricot or orange juice
½ cup (120ml) chicken or vegetable broth
1 tablespoon (15ml) extra virgin olive oil
1 tablespoon peeled and chopped fresh ginger
½ teaspoon ground cinnamon
½ teaspoon kosher salt
¼ teaspoon black pepper
3 pounds (1.4kg) sweet potatoes, peeled and
   sliced into ¼- to ½-inch-thick (6- to 12-mm)
   slices
½ cup (100g) dried apricots
½ cup (85g) pitted prunes

PREHEAT oven to 400°F (200°C).

IN A LARGE HEAVY SAUCEPAN over medium heat, bring the juice, broth, oil, ginger, cinnamon, salt, and pepper to a boil. Add the sweet potatoes and stir. Reduce the heat to medium-low, cover, and cook for 15 minutes, stirring often. Transfer the sweet potato mixture to a 9 x 13-inch (23 x 33-cm) baking dish, add the apricots and prunes, and bake, covered, for 30 minutes. Remove cover and bake for another 40 minutes, or until the sweet potatoes are tender and beginning to brown.

ASPARAGUS, ZUCCHINI, AND LEEK KUGEL
{ gebrokts }

SERVES 12–15
PREP TIME 30 minutes
COOK TIME 45 minutes
ADVANCE PREP May be made 1 day in advance
EQUIPMENT Measuring cups and spoons • Cutting board • Knives • Garlic press • Large frying pan • Tongs or silicone spatula • Box grater • 9 x 13-inch (23 x 33-cm) baking pan

I am known as the enemy of kugel because I make only one kugel every year—my grandmother's dairy recipe that appears in *The Holiday Kosher Baker*. I have stated publicly that Jewish holiday meals are heavy enough without turning our vegetables into leaden cakes. Let the record show that I have often been criticized for this opinion. But, as I keep meeting kugel lovers out there, I decided to be flexible and include this recipe. I like it because the vegetables rule the flavor.

3 tablespoons (45ml) vegetable oil
1 leek, white and light green parts only, halved and
    cut into ¼-inch-thick (6-mm) slices
1 medium onion, cut in half and thinly sliced
3 cloves garlic, crushed
1 bunch (1 pound/455g) asparagus (choose
    thicker stalks), trimmed, halved the long way,
    and cut into thirds
1 medium zucchini, not peeled, shredded on the
    large holes of a box grater (about 2 cups)
1 cup spinach leaves, stacked and sliced into
    ⅓-inch-thick (8-mm) ribbons
2 scallions, cut into ¼-inch-thick (6-mm) slices
1 tablespoon slivered fresh basil leaves (see box,
    page 56)
3 large eggs, lightly beaten

¼ cup matzoh meal
¼ teaspoon salt
Black pepper

PREHEAT oven to 375°F (190°C).

HEAT 2 tablespoons of the oil in a large frying pan over medium heat. Add the leek and onion and cook for 3 minutes. Add the garlic and asparagus and cook for another 4 minutes. Turn off the heat. Add the shredded zucchini, spinach, and scallions and stir to combine. Scoop into a large bowl and let cool for 15 minutes.

ADD the basil, eggs, matzoh meal, salt, and pepper to taste to the vegetable mixture and stir to combine. Grease a 9 x 13-inch (23 x 33-cm) baking pan with the remaining tablespoon oil. Scoop the batter into the pan and spread evenly. Bake the kugel for 45 minutes, or until browned on top.

CLEANING LEEKS

First trim the end off the white part, then remove the dark green part and discard. Slice lengthwise into the leek, through two layers, and then peel them and discard. Rinse the leek. Slice through another layer or two and open them to see if there is more dirt. If there is, rinse off the leek and then cut into the next layer to make sure it is clean. Rinse well.

INTERNATIONAL SEDER MENU

Jewish cooking has been following the "fusion" trend for centuries. As Jews have moved from place to place, we've picked up new food traditions along the way. Over the past fifteen years, I have noticed a deliberate attempt by home cooks to combine foods from many places, a trend I've observed on menus at Shabbat and holiday meals served by friends to include dishes from Israel, Latin America, and Asia. This international Seder menu is influenced by the flavors of Turkey, Morocco, France, and the United States.

MIDDLE EASTERN
CHAROSET

MAKES 3 CUPS (SERVES 25 FOR SEDER)
PREP TIME 10 minutes
ADVANCE PREP May be made 3 days in advance; add apple just before serving
EQUIPMENT Measuring cups and spoons • Food processor • Cutting board • Knives • Small serving bowl

I have always enjoyed Sephardic charoset recipes because they often taste like dessert. This recipe merges several charoset traditions and, unlike the classic Ashkenazic varieties, this one has texture.

1½ cups (230g) pitted dates
1 cup (150g) dried figs
¼ teaspoon ground nutmeg
¼ teaspoon ground ginger
2 tablespoons sweet kosher wine
1 teaspoon orange zest
    (from 1 medium orange)
1 cup (120g) walnuts, chopped into ⅓-inch
    (8-mm) pieces
1 cup (200g) dried apricots, chopped
    into ¼-inch (6-mm) pieces
1½ red apples, not peeled, chopped
    into ⅓-inch (8-mm) pieces

IN THE BOWL of a food processor fitted with a metal blade, place the dates, figs, nutmeg, ginger, wine, and zest. Process to a paste. Add the walnuts and apricots and process until the mixture comes together. Scoop into a small serving bowl; add the chopped apples and stir.

GINGERED RED PEPPER AND TOMATO SOUP

SERVES 10–12
PREP TIME 15 minutes
COOK TIME 45 minutes
ADVANCE PREP May be made 2 days in advance
EQUIPMENT Cutting board • Knives • Vegetable peeler • Measuring cups and spoons • Large soup pot • Wooden spoon • Immersion blender or food processor • Small bowl

This soup is also lovely served cold for a light lunch with avocado slices on top.

3 tablespoons (45ml) extra virgin olive oil
3 onions, cut in half and sliced into ½-inch-thick (12-mm) slices
5 cloves garlic, chopped
2-inch (5-cm) piece of fresh ginger, peeled and chopped
7 large red peppers, cut in half, seeds removed, and cut into 2-inch (5-cm) pieces
2 large fresh tomatoes, chopped
1 can (35 ounce/1kg) whole peeled tomatoes
1 quart (1L) chicken or vegetable broth
¾ cup (30g) loosely packed fresh basil leaves
Salt and white pepper (use black pepper if white is unavailable)
1 tablespoon honey

FOR THE GARNISH
2 tablespoons finely chopped red onion, cut into ¼-inch (6-mm) pieces
2 tablespoons finely chopped orange pepper, cut into ¼-inch (6-mm) pieces
2 tablespoons finely chopped yellow cherry tomatoes, cut into ¼-inch (6-mm) pieces
2 tablespoons unpeeled, finely chopped cucumber, cut into ¼-inch (6-mm) pieces

To make the soup
HEAT the oil in a large soup pot over medium-low heat. Add the onions and cook for about 8 minutes, until translucent. Add the garlic and ginger and cook for another 3 minutes. Add the peppers, tomatoes, canned tomatoes with their juices, and broth and bring to a boil. Add the basil, cover, and reduce the heat to low; simmer the soup for 45 minutes. Let cool slightly. Remove as many of the basil leaves as you can fish out, and discard.

PUREE the soup for at least 3 minutes using an immersion blender, or in batches in a food processor, until completely smooth. Season with salt and white pepper to taste. Add the honey and stir.

To make the garnish
IN A SMALL BOWL, toss the red onion, orange pepper, tomatoes, and cucumber. Top each bowl of soup with about 2 teaspoons of garnish.

> ### HONEY— THE UNIVERSAL CORRECTOR
>
> If you taste a soup, sauce, or stew after you have adjusted the flavor for salt and pepper, and it still does not taste right or seems a bit too tart or bitter, add a tablespoon of honey and stir. This performs some kind of magic that makes everything better.

SEPHARDIC POACHED FISH IN PEPPER SAUCE

SERVES 6-8
PREP TIME 10 minutes
COOK TIME 20 minutes
ADVANCE PREP May be made 3 days in advance
EQUIPMENT Cutting board • Knives • Measuring cups and spoons • Large frying pan with 2-inch (5-cm) sides • Silicone spatula

This recipe from Limor Decter is versatile and can be made with any type of white fish or salmon. You can really kick up the spice factor by adding a tablespoon of store-bought harissa sauce or some more chili powder, hot paprika, or red pepper flakes, if you like. This dish also can be served as a main course for lunch over the holiday.

3 tablespoons (45ml) extra virgin olive oil
2 cloves garlic, thinly sliced
2 medium onions, cut in half and thinly sliced
1 red pepper, cored, seeded, and thinly sliced
1 orange pepper, cored, seeded, and thinly sliced
1 yellow pepper, cored, seeded, and thinly sliced
¼ teaspoon paprika
¾ teaspoon kosher salt
Black pepper
¼–½ teaspoon chili powder, hot paprika, crushed red pepper flakes, or black pepper
1½ cups (360ml) water
2 pounds (1kg) white fish (such as tilapia, halibut, or flounder) or salmon
⅔ cup (40g) loosely packed fresh cilantro leaves, chopped

CUT fish into 2 x 5-inch (5 x 12-cm) long pieces, or fillets may be cut lengthwise in half. Set aside. Heat the oil in a large frying pan with 2-inch (5-cm) sides over medium-low heat. Add the garlic and onions and cook for 5 minutes. Add the red, orange, and yellow peppers and cook for another 4 minutes. Stir in the paprika, salt, and black pepper to taste. Stir in the chili powder. Add the water, increase the heat to medium-high, and bring to a boil.

REDUCE the heat to low, place the fish slices on top on the garlic, onions, and peppers, cover, and cook for 5 minutes. Use a fork to pick up some of the peppers and onions and place them on top of the fish slices. Cover and cook for another 5 minutes. Taste the sauce and add more salt if necessary. Sprinkle with the cilantro and serve. Serve warm or at room temperature.

VARIATIONS

- **HERBS:** Substitute fresh tarragon, basil, dill, parsley, or thyme for the cilantro, or use a combination of herbs.
- **ONIONS:** Substitute or add sliced shallots or leeks.
- **SPICES:** Add one teaspoon of cumin, curry, or your favorite spice mix.
- **FISH PIECES:** For a different look, cut the fish into cubes.

WHOLE CHICKEN WITH DRIED FRUIT STUFFING

SERVES 6-8
PREP TIME 20 minutes
COOK TIME 1¾ hours
ADVANCE PREP May be made 1 day in advance
EQUIPMENT Cutting board • Knives • Measuring cups and spoons • Large frying pan • Wooden spoon • Medium bowl • Garlic press • Large roasting pan • 8-inch (20-cm) square or other small baking pan

When I first started going on the road to do demonstrations for synagogues and Jewish organizations (way before my first baking book came out), I taught how to prepare entire meals, and I made this chicken dish all over the country. The stuffing recipe makes a generous amount, so if you are cooking for a big crowd and roast three chickens, you only need to double the stuffing recipe. During the rest of the year, I add saffron threads soaked in water (along with the water) to the stuffing, but I have yet to find any saffron threads that are certified for Passover use.

FOR THE STUFFING
1 tablespoon vegetable oil
1 large onion, chopped into ¼-inch (6-mm) pieces
3 cloves garlic, crushed
1 cup pitted prunes (175g), chopped into ½-inch (12-mm) pieces
1 cup dried apricots (200g), chopped into ⅓-inch (8-mm) pieces
¼ cup (38g) currants or raisins
1 large apple, any kind, peeled and chopped into ⅓-inch (8-cm) pieces
½ teaspoon ground turmeric
1 teaspoon ground cinnamon
¼ teaspoon salt
¼ teaspoon black pepper

FOR THE CHICKEN
1 large whole chicken
2 tablespoons (30ml) extra virgin olive oil
1 teaspoon ground turmeric
Salt and black pepper

To make the stuffing
IN A LARGE FRYING PAN, heat the oil over medium heat. Add the onion and garlic and cook for 8 minutes, or until they begin to brown. Add the prunes, apricots, currants, apple, turmeric, cinnamon, salt, and pepper and stir. Cook for 3 minutes, stirring occasionally. Transfer to a medium bowl and let cool for 10 minutes.

To make the chicken
PREHEAT oven to 450°F (230°C).

PLACE the chicken in a roasting pan. Stuff as much of the dried fruit mixture as you can fit into the cavity of the chicken. Place any leftover stuffing in a small baking dish, cover with aluminum foil, and set aside. Drizzle 1 tablespoon of the oil over the chicken, sprinkle with ½ teaspoon of the turmeric, and season with salt and pepper to taste. Use gloves, or cover your hand with a small plastic bag, and rub the oil and turmeric all over the chicken. Turn the chicken

~ continued ~

ROASTING WHOLE CHICKENS

Whole chickens cook best when you roast them breast side down first and then turn them over for the remaining cooking time. It is useful to have kitchen scissors on hand to cut a whole chicken into pieces for serving.

over. Add the other tablespoon oil, the remaining ½ teaspoon turmeric, and more salt and pepper; rub all over the chicken. Leave the chicken, breast side down, in the roasting pan.

ROAST the chicken for 20 minutes. Carefully turn the chicken over and roast, breast side up, for another 20 minutes. Reduce the heat to 350°F (180°C). Add the covered pan of extra stuffing to the oven. Roast the chicken and bake the stuffing for 50 minutes more, or until the juices run clear when you pierce the chicken with a fork. Let the chicken sit for 5 minutes and then cut it into pieces for serving. Scoop the stuffing out of the chicken and combine it with the stuffing that was cooked separately. Serve the chicken pieces over the stuffing and drizzle some of the pan juices on top.

MOROCCAN SPICED SHORT RIBS

SERVES 6
PREP TIME 5 minutes for spice rub, marinate meat for 8 hours or overnight
COOK TIME 10 minutes to sear meat, 2½ hours to bake
ADVANCE PREP May be made 3 days in advance
EQUIPMENT Measuring spoons • 9 x 13-inch (23 x 33-cm) baking pan • Small bowl • Tongs • Large heavy frying pan or outdoor grill

Of all the main course dishes that I serve to my three sons, this is the one they always request before they go away to camp and on the first Shabbat after their return. You can easily double this recipe for a crowd. I use my grill to sear the meat, but you can sear it in a heavy pan on the stovetop. Be sure to bake the short ribs until you can easily slide a fork into the meat.

4 long strips (3½–4 pounds/1.5–2kg) top rib (flanken)
1 tablespoon light brown sugar
1 tablespoon ground cumin
1 teaspoon ground turmeric
1 teaspoon ground thyme
1 teaspoon ground cinnamon
½ teaspoon salt
½ teaspoon black pepper, plus more to taste
2 teaspoons extra virgin olive oil, for searing the meat in a pan
¾ cup (180ml) barbeque sauce
⅓ cup (75ml) hot water

PLACE meat in a 9 x 13-inch (23 x 33-cm) baking pan. In a small bowl, mix the brown sugar, cumin, turmeric, thyme, cinnamon, salt, and pepper until well combined. Rub the spice mix all over all sides of the meat. Cover the pan with plastic wrap and refrigerate for at least 8 hours or overnight.

PREHEAT oven to 325°F (160°C).

YOU CAN MAKE THESE SHORT RIBS TWO WAYS. To make them on an outdoor grill, heat the grill to high heat, 550° to 600°F (280° to 300°C). Sear each side until the meat releases on its own, about 5 to 7 minutes per side, then return the ribs to the baking pan. To make the ribs on the stovetop, heat the oil in a large heavy frying pan over medium-high heat and brown the meat on all sides.

COMBINE the barbeque sauce and water in a small bowl and pour it over the meat. Season with pepper to taste. Cover the pan with aluminum foil and bake the meat for 2½ hours. If you've made the meat in advance and it is cold, remove the fat from the top before reheating. To serve, cut the ribs into 3-inch (7-cm) pieces. To reheat, use a fork to remove the fat from the meat and heat at 350°F (180°C) for 35 minutes.

CLOCKWISE FROM TOP
Moroccan Spiced Short Ribs, opposite;
Parsnip and Apple Puree, page 25;
Brussels Sprouts and Shallots, page 24.

ROASTED VEGETABLES WITH TARRAGON

SERVES 10
PREP TIME 15 minutes
COOK TIME 17 minutes
ADVANCE PREP May be made 2 days in advance
EQUIPMENT Cutting board • Knives • Measuring spoons • Garlic press • Vegetable peeler • Large roasting pan • Large spoon

You can vary this recipe every time you prepare it, depending on what ingredients are sitting in your fridge. See what vegetables you need to use up before you go shopping.

1 large parsnip
1 large sweet potato
1 large fennel bulb, stalk and leaves trimmed off
1 large red or yellow pepper
1 medium eggplant
½ head cauliflower, cut into florets
1 red onion, cut into ½-inch (12-mm) pieces
3 tablespoons (45ml) extra virgin olive oil
6 cloves garlic, crushed
¼ teaspoon black pepper
4 teaspoons chopped fresh tarragon leaves
Salt

PREHEAT oven to broil. Place an oven rack at the upper middle of the oven.

CUT the parsnip, sweet potato, fennel, and red pepper into 1½-inch (4-cm) pieces; place them in a roasting pan. Cut the eggplant into 2-inch (5-cm) pieces and add to the pan along with the caulifower florets. Add the onion pieces and toss to combine. Add the oil, garlic, and pepper and toss gently.

BROIL the vegetable mixture for 7 minutes. Stir the vegetables, making sure that the browned pieces end up on the bottom. Broil for another 7 minutes and stir again. Broil for a final 3 minutes, or until parsnip pieces are fork-tender. (You want the vegetables to be a little bit firm.) Remove the pan from the oven, add the tarragon and salt to taste, and toss. Serve warm or at room temperature.

BRUSSELS SPROUTS AND SHALLOTS

SERVES 6
PREP TIME 10 minutes
COOK TIME 20 minutes
ADVANCE PREP May be made 1 day in advance
EQUIPMENT Cutting board • Knives • Measuring spoons • Jelly roll or roasting pan

Brussels sprouts have become very trendy over the past few years, a fact that amazes my parents, who grew up hating them. Roasting vegetables in the oven is a great way to retain their nutrition and keep them crisp. My children fight over these Brussels sprouts, especially the crunchy leaves that blacken into chips during roasting.

2 pounds (1kg) Brussels sprouts, trimmed, outer leaves removed, cut in half
4 small shallots, halved and cut lengthwise into ¼-inch-thick (6-mm) slices
2 tablespoons extra virgin olive oil
Salt and black pepper

PREHEAT oven to 425°F (220°C).

LINE a jelly roll pan with aluminum foil or use a roasting pan. Place the Brussels sprouts and

PARSNIP AND APPLE PUREE

SERVES 6-8
PREP TIME 10 minutes
COOK TIME 30 minutes
ADVANCE PREP May be made 3 days in advance
EQUIPMENT Measuring cups and spoons • Cutting board • Knives • Vegetable peeler • Medium saucepan • Immersion blender or food processor

French chefs adore serving purees made from every vegetable imaginable. That is probably why the homemade baby food for my first two children, who were born in Europe, consisted at times of pureed fennel, pumpkin, and artichoke. This recipe for parsnip and apple puree is a creamy and lighter alternative to mashed potatoes. My kids never tire of potatoes during Passover, but I do (or perhaps my waistline does).

6 parsnips, peeled and cut into 1-inch
   (2.5-cm) slices
2 tablespoons (30ml) extra virgin olive oil
¾ cup (180ml) water
2 red apples (any kind), peeled, cored,
   and cut into 2-inch (5-cm) pieces
2 sprigs fresh rosemary

PLACE the parsnips, oil, water, apples, and rosemary in a medium saucepan and cook, covered, over medium-low heat until soft, approximately 30 minutes. Remove the rosemary sprig and most of the leaves, but keep in just a few leaves. In a food processor fitted with a metal blade, puree the parsnip and apple mixture until smooth, or use an immersion blender right in the saucepan.

CLEANING BRUSSELS SPROUTS

There are different rules about how to clean and inspect Brussels sprouts to ensure that they are bug-free and kosher. Please check with your rabbinic authority for precise directions. See page 68 for my technique.

shallots on top of the foil. Add the oil and toss to combine. Roast for 20 minutes, or until the Brussels sprouts are browned and fork-tender, stirring twice during roasting. Add salt and pepper to taste.

SHABBAT MENU

After preparing all the dishes and ritual foods for the Seder, cooking Shabbat dinner during Passover does not seem so daunting. Some years, Shabbat will overlap with Yom Tov, and you can use this menu then as well—it is full of the recipes I make all year long. The Seder Plate Salad is, however, a new creation, but I think it will appear on my porch as a Shabbat lunch dish this summer.

CARAMELIZED ONION AND SWEET POTATO SOUP

SERVES 10
PREP TIME 20 minutes
COOK TIME 1 hour, 20 minutes
ADVANCE PREP May be made 3 days in advance
EQUIPMENT Cutting board • Knives • Measuring cups and spoons • Large soup pot • Wooden spoon • Immersion blender or food processor

This is one of the Shoyer family's favorite soups and the one I serve every Thanksgiving. It was created years ago by necessity. I was making a pureed French onion soup and discovered I had no white potatoes. I added sweet potatoes instead, and thus this creamy soup recipe was born. Once at a conference in Baltimore, a woman ran up to me and said that this soup had replaced chicken soup as her family's Friday night soup. Make sure to brown the onions really well without burning them; the more caramelized they are, the more flavorful the soup will be.

¼ cup (60ml) vegetable oil
4 pounds (2kg) onions, halved and cut into
    1-inch-thick (2.5-cm) slices
4 cloves garlic, roughly chopped
½ teaspoon salt, or more as needed
¼ teaspoon white pepper (use black pepper
    if white is unavailable), or more as needed
3 large sweet potatoes, cut into 2-inch (5-cm)
    chunks
2 quarts (2L) vegetable or chicken broth
    or water

HEAT the oil in a large soup pot over high heat. Add the onions and cook, stirring often, until they are well browned, about 40 minutes. If the onions start to stick on the bottom of the pot, just stir them. You want the onions to be nicely browned, not burned.

ADD the garlic, salt, and pepper and cook for 5 minutes more. Add the sweet potatoes and broth. Bring to a boil and then simmer for 40 minutes, or until the potatoes are soft. Cool slightly.

PUREE the soup, using an immersion blender for 3 full minutes, or in batches in a food processor, until it is completely smooth.

THE CREAMIEST PUREED SOUP

While testing recipes for Susie Fishbein's *Kosher by Design Entertains* cookbook, I learned from Susie that if you puree soup for 3 full minutes it gets much creamier than if you puree just until the vegetables appear smooth.

SMOTHERED CHICKEN
WITH WINE AND HERBS

SERVES 10
PREP TIME 20 minutes
COOK TIME 1 hour, 10 minutes
ADVANCE PREP May be made 2 days in advance
EQUIPMENT Cutting board • Knives • Measuring
cups and spoons • Shallow bowl • Large saucepan
with 2-inch (5-cm) sides • Tongs • Large roasting
pan • Wooden spoon

Every Passover my brothers and I could rely on
the dishes my mother prepared every single year.
This is an updated version of her recipe for a
tasty chicken stew, which I believe she found
in a Jewish newspaper back in the 1970s.

½–1 cup (80–160g) potato starch or matzoh
   cake meal (65g–130g)
¼ cup (60ml) extra virgin olive oil, plus
   up to 2 tablespoons more if needed
2 large whole chickens, cut into 8 pieces
Salt and black pepper
2 large onions, chopped into ½-inch (1-cm) pieces
3 stalks celery, cut into ⅓-inch (8-mm) cubes
4 large carrots, peeled and cut into ⅓-inch
   (8-mm) cubes
5 cloves garlic, roughly chopped
6 fresh sage leaves
6 fresh basil leaves
½ cup (120ml) white wine
Leaves of 6 sprigs thyme, or 1 teaspoon dried
   thyme

PREHEAT oven to 375°F (190°C).

PLACE the potato starch in a shallow bowl. In a
large saucepan with 2-inch (5-cm) sides, heat the
oil over high heat. (If you are using a dark-colored
pan, cook over medium-high heat.) Sprinkle the
chicken pieces with salt and pepper and then dip
them into the potato starch to coat, shaking off
any excess. Cook in batches until golden brown
on both sides, about 4 minutes per side. Place
the browned pieces in a large roasting pan, skin
side up.

ADD the chopped onions, celery, and carrots to
the saucepan and cook for 5 minutes, scraping
the bottom of the pan to loosen any chicken fat
or pieces and mix them in. If the saucepan looks
dry, add another 1 or 2 tablespoons oil. Add the
garlic and cook for another 2 minutes. Meanwhile,
on a cutting board, chop the sage and basil leaves
into small pieces. Add the wine to the pan and
cook, stirring often, until the wine is almost all
evaporated. Add salt and pepper to taste.

POUR the cooked vegetables over the chicken
pieces. Sprinkle with the sage, basil, and thyme,
cover, and bake for 1 hour. Uncover and bake for
another 10 minutes to allow the chicken pieces
to brown a little on top. Serve in a bowl, with the
vegetables on top of the chicken pieces.

WASHING
FRESH HERBS

Fill a salad spinner or bowl with cold
water. Submerge the herbs in the water
and swish them around to loosen any
dirt. Lift the herbs out of the water and
look at the water. If the water is clean,
the herbs are clean. If the water is dirty,
dump it out, rinse the salad spinner or
bowl, and repeat until the water is clean.

SEDER PLATE SALAD

SERVES 6
PREP TIME 10 minutes
COOK TIME 10 minutes
ADVANCE PREP Dressing and lamb may be made 2 days in advance
EQUIPMENT Cutting board • Knives • Measuring cups and spoons • Small saucepan • Tongs • Small bowl • Whisk • Large serving bowl

This is my version of a French Niçoise salad. I make it with lamb instead of tuna, and it contains the ritual components of the Seder plate and table. The dressing is made from kosher sweet wine and *maror* (the bitter herb, in this case, white horseradish), creating a creamy pink dressing. This salad also makes a nice lunch or light dinner during *chol hamoed*, the nonholiday days of Passover.

FOR THE SALAD

2 pieces of lamb shoulder (about 20 ounces/ 600g total)
2 teaspoons extra virgin olive oil
Salt and black pepper
1 large head romaine lettuce, cut into 2-inch (5-cm) pieces
2 stalks celery, thinly sliced
1 cup (40g) loosely packed fresh parsley leaves, roughly chopped
⅓ cup (40g) walnut halves, roughly chopped into ½-inch (12-mm) pieces
2 apples (Red Delicious, Fuji, or Gala), cored and cut into ¾-inch (2-cm) cubes
3 large eggs, hard-boiled and quartered (see page 4)

FOR THE DRESSING

½ cup (120ml) mayonnaise
4 teaspoons jarred white horseradish
1 tablespoon sugar
2 tablespoons sweet kosher wine
Salt and black pepper

PREHEAT oven to broil or an outdoor grill to medium-high heat.

To make the lamb
RUB the lamb with oil and sprinkle with salt and pepper to taste. Broil or grill for 4 to 5 minutes per side for medium rare, or until desired doneness. Let cool for 5 minutes and, if serving immediately, slice into thin, 2-inch-long (5-cm) pieces. If making in advance, wait to slice the lamb until after reheating. The lamb may be roasted 2 days in advance; cover and store in the fridge.

To make the salad dressing

IN A SMALL BOWL, whisk the mayonnaise, white horseradish, sugar, and wine until well combined. Add salt and pepper to taste. The dressing may be made 2 days in advance; cover and store in the fridge.

To assemble the salad

PLACE the romaine pieces in a large bowl. Add the celery and parsley and toss to combine. Sprinkle the walnuts and apples on top and arrange the egg quarters around the perimeter of the bowl. Scatter the lamb pieces on top. To serve, scoop some of everything onto each plate and drizzle with the dressing.

GARLIC AND ROSEMARY MASHED POTATOES

SERVES 8

PREP TIME 15 minutes

COOK TIME 20 minutes

ADVANCE PREP May be made 2 days in advance

EQUIPMENT Measuring cups and spoons • Medium saucepan • Small saucepan • Potato masher • Small sieve • Vegetable peeler • Cutting board • Knives • Slotted spoon • Large bowl

I find that if I serve potatoes and chocolate in some form (although not together) to my children every day during Passover, they do not complain about missing pasta and bagels. Mashed potatoes are ideally served the day they are made. To reheat the next day, add another 2 tablespoons margarine and a little salt, reheat, and then mash everything together. When making these potatoes in advance, store them in a large bowl so that when you reheat them you'll have room to mix and soften them well.

4 large russet potatoes

1 teaspoon kosher salt

¼ cup (60ml) extra virgin olive oil

8 large cloves garlic, peeled

1 large sprig fresh rosemary

3 tablespoons (42g) margarine

Salt and black pepper

PEEL and cut the potatoes into 2- to 3-inch (5- to 7-cm) chunks. Place in a medium saucepan and add water to cover. Bring to a boil, add the salt, cover, and cook over medium heat until fork-tender, 15 to 20 minutes.

MEANWHILE, place the oil in a small saucepan. Add the garlic and heat over medium heat until it sizzles. Add the rosemary, reduce the heat to low, and cook until soft, about 15 minutes. Every once in a while, turn the garlic pieces over so they do not brown too much on one side. Turn off the heat and let sit until the potatoes are ready.

USE a slotted spoon to scoop up a quarter of the potatoes into a large bowl. Do not discard the starchy cooking water. Add two of the garlic cloves and use a potato masher to mash the potatoes and garlic together. Add another quarter of the potatoes and two more garlic cloves and mash. Add 3 tablespoons of the starchy water and mash it in.

USE a small sieve to strain half the cooking oil into the potatoes and mash to combine. Add the remaining potatoes and garlic in two parts, along with the remaining oil. Add the margarine and salt and pepper to taste and mix well.

ROASTED ASPARAGUS WITH TOASTED ALMOND AND ORANGE GREMOLATA

SERVES 8
PREP TIME 10 minutes
COOK TIME 16 minutes
ADVANCE PREP May be made 1 day in advance
EQUIPMENT Cutting board • Knives • Measuring cups and spoons • Garlic press • Zester • Cookie sheet or frying pan • Small saucepan • Silicone spatula

Gremolata is a combination of chopped herbs, garlic, and lemon peel that is typically added to veal osso buco. It may be made with other ingredients as well. Here it is prepared with orange zest and nuts and sprinkled on asparagus.

2 pounds (900g) asparagus spears
4 teaspoons extra virgin olive oil, divided
¼ cup (25g) sliced almonds
2 large cloves garlic, crushed
1 teaspoon orange zest (from 1 orange)
Salt and black pepper

PREHEAT oven to 400°F (200°C).

TRIM the asparagus and place on a lined baking sheet. Add 2 teaspoons of the oil and toss to coat. Roast for 15 minutes, or until fork-tender. Alternatively, you can cook the asparagus in a large frying pan. Heat the pan with an inch of water, bring to a boil, add the asparagus, and cook until fork-tender, about 5 minutes; drain and dry the asparagus.

MEANWHILE, to make the gremolata, place a small saucepan over medium-low heat and add the almonds. Stir often until toasted. Watch them carefully so they do not burn. Add the remaining 2 teaspoons oil, the garlic, and the orange zest, and stir. Cook for 1 minute and then set aside to cool.

WHEN THE ASPARAGUS SPEARS are cooked, move them to a platter. Add salt and pepper to taste. Scatter the gremolata on top and serve warm or at room temperature.

TOASTING NUTS

ON THE STOVETOP: Heat a frying pan over medium heat, add the nuts and stir often until golden brown on all sides. Do not walk away because the nuts may burn the second you do.

IN THE OVEN: Preheat oven to 325°F (160°C). Place the nuts on a cookie sheet and bake for 15 to 20 minutes, shaking the pan or stirring once, until golden brown and fragrant.

YOM TOV MENU

This is a fresh, colorful menu to serve during the last days of Passover, when cooking fatigue starts to set in. These dishes will wake up all your senses. During holidays and Shabbat, when I have more than fifteen guests, I serve the main course on a buffet so that guests do not have to pass around heavy serving bowls or end up with food that is less hot than desirable.

ZUCCHINI BASIL SOUP

SERVES 14

PREP TIME 15 minutes

COOK TIME 1 hour

ADVANCE PREP May be made 3 days in advance or frozen

EQUIPMENT Measuring cups and spoons • Cutting board • Knives • Large soup pot • Silicone spatula or wooden spoon • Immersion blender or food processor

This is a very healthy, velvety soup. By adding the fresh spinach at the end of the cooking time, you retain its nutrients and turn the soup a beautiful shade of green.

¼ cup (60ml) extra virgin olive oil

3 large onions, halved and cut into ½-inch-thick (12-mm) slices

5 cloves garlic, roughly chopped

8 large zucchini, trimmed, not peeled

10 cups (2.5L) chicken or vegetable broth

⅛ teaspoon white pepper (use black pepper if white is unavailable), plus more if needed

Salt

12 large fresh basil leaves

2 large handfuls baby spinach leaves (about 5 loosely packed cups/130g)

IN A LARGE SOUP POT, heat the oil over medium heat. Add the onions and cook for 10 minutes, stirring often, until the onions are translucent but not browned. Add the garlic and cook for another 2 minutes.

MEANWHILE, cut off one-third of one zucchini, cut it into ½-inch (12-mm) cubes, and set aside. Cut the rest of the zucchini in half the long way, and then cut it into ¾-inch-thick (2-cm) slices.

WHEN THE ONIONS AND GARLIC ARE COOKED, add the zucchini slices, broth, pepper, and some salt to taste, and bring to a boil. Add 6 of the basil leaves, reduce the heat to a simmer, cover, and simmer for 30 minutes, or until the vegetables are soft. Add the spinach, reserved zucchini cubes, and the remaining 6 basil leaves, and turn off the heat. Let the soup sit, covered, for 10 minutes. Use an immersion blender and puree for 3 full minutes, or use a food processor to puree the soup in batches. Taste for seasoning, adding more salt and pepper if necessary.

PUREED SOUP SCIENCE

I teach baking classes in my home, but every once in a while I also teach a "science of soup" class. In this class, I show my students how to create their own pureed soups:

Start with some fat, add onion, garlic, shallots or leeks, any spices, and, after a few minutes, 2 pounds (1kg) of a vegetable, cover with broth, bring to a boil, cook until done, and puree. Armed with these basics, you can create your own signature soups.

BEET AND BUTTERNUT SQUASH SALAD

SERVES 8
PREP TIME 15 minutes; cool beets for 30 minutes
COOK TIME 1 hour
ADVANCE PREP Salad dressing, beets, and squash may be prepared 2 days in advance
EQUIPMENT Cutting board • Knives • Measuring cups and spoons • Medium bowl • Zester • Jelly roll or roasting pan • 2 small bowls • Whisk

I was always concerned about the high sugar content of beets until I learned that they have the ability to lower blood pressure, reduce inflammation, detoxify your liver, and ward off cancer, while adding fiber to your diet. These benefits, plus great flavor, are all the reasons you need to add beets to your diet all year round. This is a vibrant salad, whether served in a large bowl or plated.

FOR THE SALAD

3 medium red beets
3 medium golden beets
2 cups (280g) diced butternut squash,
   1-inch (2.5-cm) cubes
2 teaspoons extra virgin olive oil
5 ounces (140g) arugula leaves
   (about 6 cups/120g)
1 cup loosely packed fresh cilantro leaves,
   roughly chopped
⅓ cup (60g) pomegranate seeds
   (from 1 pomegranate), for garnish

FOR THE DRESSING

2 tablespoons (30ml) extra virgin olive oil
2 teaspoons balsamic vinegar
1 teaspoon orange zest (from 1 orange)

CUBING WHOLE BUTTERNUT SQUASH

If you cannot find butternut squash already peeled and cubed at a kosher store, buy a whole squash and use a vegetable peeler to remove as much of the outer, dark skin as possible. This will make it easier to cut the squash.

1 teaspoon fresh orange juice (from zested orange)
¼ teaspoon salt, plus more as needed
Black pepper

To make the salad
PREHEAT oven to 400°F (200°C).

TRIM the beets, then rinse, dry, and wrap each beet in aluminum foil. Place the beets on one side of a jelly roll or roasting pan. Place the butternut squash cubes on the other side of the pan, drizzle them with the oil, and toss to coat.

BAKE the beets and squash for 20 minutes, or until the squash cubes are fork-tender. Remove the pan from the oven and transfer the roasted squash cubes to a medium bowl to cool. Return the beets to the oven and roast for another 30 to 40 minutes, or until the center of the beets can be pierced with a fork. Let cool on the pan for 30 minutes, or until cool enough to handle.

PLACE the arugula leaves in a large serving bowl and toss with the cilantro. Add the butternut squash cubes.

~ continued ~

To make the dressing

IN A SMALL BOWL, whisk the oil, balsamic vinegar, orange zest and juice, and salt and pepper to taste until combined. Taste to see if more salt or black pepper is needed.

WHEN THE BEETS ARE COOL, put on gloves and unwrap the golden beets first. You will be able to slide the peels off them. Cut the golden beets into 1- to 1½-inch (2.5- to 4-cm) cubes and scatter them over the greens. Unwrap the red beets, remove the peels, and cut into the 1- to 1½-inch (2.5- to 4-cm) cubes; scatter them over the salad. Whisk the dressing again, drizzle over the salad, and toss. Scatter the pomegranate seeds on top.

LAMB STEW WITH APRICOTS, PEAR, AND MINT

SERVES 8
PREP TIME 20 minutes
COOK TIME 2 hours, 10 minutes
ADVANCE PREP May be made 2 days in advance
EQUIPMENT Cutting board • Knives • Measuring cups and spoons • Zester • Large wide saucepan and baking pan or Dutch oven • Tongs • Wooden spoon • Pan for toasting nuts

Moti Yitzhaky was an auto mechanic before he opened Moti's Market and Grill in Rockville, Maryland, which now provides our community with a full-service kosher butcher, baker, and grocery store, all in one. He applies the same precision from his former career to recipe development and has created flavorful food inspired by his Moroccan ancestry and beyond. Moti gave me a recipe that was the inspiration for this one, a hearty stew brightened up for spring with fresh pear and mint.

2 tablespoons (30ml) extra virgin olive oil, divided
3 pounds boneless lamb, cut into 1½-inch (4-cm) pieces
2 medium onions, cut in half and thinly sliced
6 cloves garlic, roughly chopped
2 teaspoons lemon zest (from 1 lemon)
⅓ cup (80ml) fresh orange juice (from 1 orange)
1 cinnamon stick
1 tablespoon honey
2 cups (480ml) beef, chicken, or vegetable broth
¼ teaspoon salt
⅛ teaspoon black pepper
6 ounces (170g) dried apricots
½ cup (45g) sliced almonds, toasted (see box page 34)
1 large pear, not peeled, cut into 2-inch (5-cm) cubes
¼ cup (15g) chopped fresh mint leaves

IN A LARGE WIDE SAUCEPAN OR DUTCH OVEN, heat 1 tablespoon of the oil over medium-high heat. Add the lamb pieces in batches and cook, using tongs to turn the pieces, until well browned on all sides. Do not crowd the pan. Remove the browned pieces to a large bowl. Add the onions and garlic to the saucepan plus the other tablespoon of oil and cook, scraping the bottom of the saucepan to avoid sticking, for 5 minutes, until the onions are browned. If the onions start to burn, turn the heat down to medium.

ADD THE LEMON ZEST, orange juice, cinnamon stick, honey, and broth to the saucepan and bring to a boil. Season with salt and pepper to taste. Return the lamb pieces to the saucepan, cover, and cook on low heat for 1½ hours.

ADD THE APRICOTS, almonds, and pear cubes to the pan, stir, and cook for another 40 minutes. Add the mint, stir, and serve.

COCONUT SCHNITZEL WITH ALMOND BUTTER SAUCE

SERVES 8
PREP TIME 20 minutes
COOK TIME 25 minutes
ADVANCE PREP Sauce may be made 3 days in advance; chicken is best eaten the same day, but may be made 1 day in advance
EQUIPMENT Measuring cups and spoons • Medium bowl or 2-cup (480-ml) liquid measuring cup • Whisk • 3 shallow bowls • Cutting board • Knives • Garlic press • Large frying pan • Jelly roll pan or cookie sheet • Tongs

When almond butter for Passover appeared on the market a few years ago, my first thought was, what dessert can I make with it? What I ultimately came up with was a mock peanut sauce to be used as part of this main dish. You may also serve the schnitzel straight, or with your favorite BBQ or other nut-free sauce.

CUTTING CHICKEN SLICES

Some kosher butchers sell chicken scaloppini slices. If you can only get the thicker, boneless pieces, you can slice them laterally to create slices that are 2 x 5 x 1/3 inch thick (5cm x 12cm x 8mm). Another option is to take the boneless chicken breasts and pound them between two pieces of waxed paper; I use a saucepan or frying pan to do the pounding.

FOR THE SAUCE

1/2 cup (120ml) almond butter
3/4 cup (180ml) boiling water
1 clove garlic, crushed
1 tablespoon cider vinegar
1 tablespoon finely chopped red onion
1 tablespoon sugar
Salt and black pepper

FOR THE CHICKEN

1 1/2–2 pounds (750g–1kg) chicken scaloppini (or see box below)
1/2 cup (65g) matzoh cake meal or potato starch (80g)
3 large eggs, beaten
3/4 cup matzoh meal, Passover crumbs, or Passover panko
1 cup (85g) dried coconut flakes (not shredded coconut), not toasted
2 teaspoons garlic powder
1/4 teaspoon salt
1/2 teaspoon black pepper
3 tablespoons (45ml) vegetable oil, or more as needed

To make the sauce
IN A MEDIUM BOWL or 2-cup (480-ml) liquid measuring cup, whisk the almond butter and boiling water until smooth. Add the garlic, vinegar, red onion, sugar, and salt and pepper to taste, and whisk well. May be made 3 days in advance; cover and store in the fridge. Serve at room temperature.

To make the chicken
PREHEAT oven to 300°F (150°C).

PLACE the cake meal in one shallow bowl and the eggs in a second shallow bowl. In a third shallow bowl, mix the matzoh meal, coconut flakes, garlic

powder, salt, and pepper until well combined. Heat 2 tablespoons of the oil in a large frying pan over medium-high heat. Dip both sides of each piece of chicken into the cake meal, then dip each piece into the beaten eggs and, finally, into the coconut breading.

WORKING in batches, cook each piece of chicken for 2 to 3 minutes per side, or until golden. The pieces do not need to be completely cooked through; just cook until golden. Do not crowd the pan. As each piece finishes browning, remove to a baking sheet. When the pan seems dry, add the remaining tablespoon oil, plus more if needed. When all the chicken has been cooked, place in the oven for 10 minutes. Serve the chicken with the almond butter sauce on the side.

CAULIFLOWER SLABS
WITH BASIL PESTO

SERVES 6–8
PREP TIME 10 minutes
COOK TIME 40–45 minutes
ADVANCE PREP May be made 2 days in advance
EQUIPMENT Cutting board • Knives • Measuring cups and spoons • Jelly roll or large shallow roasting pan • Food processor or blender • Silicone spatula

Every year my mother, Toby Marcus, fries cauliflower dipped in egg and matzoh meal to create a crunchy side dish. This recipe is lighter and healthier, although I always hope that my mother will make the fried version for me. The idea here is to cut large slices of the cauliflower head and then use any crumbs that fall off in the pesto topping.

FOR THE CAULIFLOWER
4 tablespoons (60ml) extra virgin olive oil, divided
1 large head (or 2 small ones) cauliflower
½ teaspoon kosher salt
Black pepper

FOR THE PESTO
1 cup cauliflower "crumbs," collected after slicing the head
12 large basil leaves
3 cloves garlic
1 teaspoon fresh lemon juice (from 1 lemon)
⅔ cup (160ml) extra virgin olive oil
Salt and black pepper

To make the cauliflower
PREHEAT oven to 425°F (220°C).

LINE a jelly roll pan with aluminum foil or use a large shallow roasting pan. Pour 2 tablespoons of the oil onto the pan and spread it around to cover the bottom.

REMOVE the outer green leaves from the cauliflower. Rinse well and trim off any dirty spots. Using a long, sharp knife, slice the head in half from stem to top of the head. Cut ¾-inch-thick (2-cm) slices, from the top of the head to the stem end, and place them on the pan, one at a time. Some of the pieces that fall off onto the cutting board will stay intact, but the smaller pieces may crumble. Place any pieces that are 1-inch (2.5-cm) or larger on the pan, along with the cauliflower slices. Pick out the smaller cauliflower pieces (you should have about 1 cup) and place them in the bowl of a food processor.

DRIZZLE the remaining 2 tablespoons oil over the cauliflower on the pan. Sprinkle with the salt and season with pepper to taste. Roast for 20 minutes.

To make the pesto
MEANWHILE, add the basil, garlic, lemon juice, and some salt and pepper to the cauliflower pieces in the processor bowl. Process until the cauliflower and basil are finely chopped. With the machine running, slowly pour the olive oil into the processor bowl. Use a silicone spatula to scrape down any pieces that are stuck to the sides of the bowl.

AFTER THE CAULIFLOWER HAS COOKED for 15 minutes and is a little browned, spread the pesto on top of the slabs. Reduce oven temperature to 375°F (190°C) and cook for another 5 to 10 minutes, or until fork-tender.

SPINACH WITH APPLES AND RAISINS

SERVES 6–8
PREP TIME 5 minutes
COOK TIME 15 minutes
ADVANCE PREP May be made 1 day in advance
EQUIPMENT Measuring cups and spoons • Cutting board • Knives • Large frying pan with at least 2-inch (5-cm) sides or saucepan • Tongs • Silicone spatula

This dish is popular on both Italian and Spanish menus and is a great way to serve spinach to people who find it boring. I like to cook spinach until it is just wilted, as shown below left, but you can cook it longer if you prefer softer spinach.

¼ cup (60ml) extra virgin olive oil
6 cloves garlic, chopped
2 red apples (any kind), not peeled, cut into 1-inch (2.5-cm) cubes
⅓ cup (55g) raisins
10 ounces (275g) baby spinach leaves
1½ teaspoons kosher salt
Black pepper

HEAT the oil in a large frying pan over medium-high heat. Add the garlic and apples and cook for 4 minutes, or until they start to brown. Add the raisins and stir.

ADD the spinach leaves in four batches, using tongs to move the cooked leaves to the top of the pile and the uncooked spinach leaves to the bottom of the pan, until most of the leaves are wilted, about 30 to 40 seconds per batch. Add the next batch of spinach.

WHEN THE SPINACH IS ALMOST ALL WILTED, season with salt and pepper, and toss. Serve warm.

SPAGHETTI SQUASH FRITTERS
{ gebrokts }

MAKES 12–14 FRITTERS

PREP TIME 15 minutes

COOK TIME 45 minutes for squash plus time to cool, 20 minutes for fritters

ADVANCE PREP Squash may be baked 1 day in advance; fritters may be made 3 days in advance

EQUIPMENT Jelly roll pan • Cutting board • Knives • Measuring cups and spoons • Large bowl • Colander with small holes • Large frying pan • Silicone spatula • Cooling rack

I learned to cook spaghetti squash from the original *Moosewood Cookbook*, which was probably the first non-Hadassah or sisterhood cookbook I ever used. At the time, I marveled at Mollie Katzen's recipes, which elevated vegetables into spectacular main courses. These fritters are similar to latkes.

1 large spaghetti squash

2 large eggs

1 tablespoon peeled, chopped fresh ginger

2 shallots, chopped into ¼-inch-thick (6-mm) pieces

1½ teaspoons ground cumin

½ teaspoon ground ginger

¾ teaspoon ground cinnamon

2 teaspoons lemon zest (from 1 lemon)

¼ teaspoon ground turmeric

⅓ cup (45g) matzoh meal

½ cup (80g) potato starch

1½ teaspoons kosher salt

⅛ teaspoon black pepper

Vegetable oil for frying

PREHEAT oven to 350°F (180°C).

PLACE the whole squash on a jelly roll pan and bake for 45 minutes, or until you can pierce it with a fork. Let cool. Slice lengthwise in half and use a fork or your hands to scrape the strands into a bowl. The squash may be baked 1 day in advance and stored in the fridge.

USE your hands to squeeze clumps of spaghetti squash strands over a colander several times to get out as much moisture as possible. Place the squash strands on a dish towel or paper towels to absorb more moisture.

IN A LARGE BOWL, place the eggs, fresh ginger, shallots, cumin, ground ginger, cinnamon, lemon zest, turmeric, matzoh meal, potato starch, salt, and black pepper and mix well. Add the squash strands and mix. If the mixture is still very wet, drain the squash mixture over a colander and squeeze it a few times. Return to the bowl.

POUR ½ inch (12-mm) oil into a large frying pan and heat over medium-high heat. When the oil is hot, spoon 2-tablespoon clumps of batter into the pan and use a spoon to press the clumps down. (Do not crowd the pan.) Fry until the squash fritters are very brown and crisp, and then turn them over and fry until they are well browned. Transfer the fritters to a cooling rack placed over a piece of aluminum foil. Repeat with the remaining batter. If the batter gets too wet halfway through frying, drain again. Serve warm.

FRENCH DAIRY MENU

n the 1990s, I was fortunate to live in Geneva, Switzerland, for four years and enjoyed my time eating throughout nearby France, where food is extremely seasonal. This menu reflects my favorite dishes on the French food calendar. In the summertime, eggplant and zucchini are at their peak, and ratatouille is served everywhere. The fall kale salad is my healthy addition to the menu. Once the winter starts, gratins (pronounced *gratan*)—vegetables and roots baked in cream and cheese—are very popular. As the weather gets nicer in the spring, tuna stews are replaced with lighter seared tuna dishes. My family loves the way all these dishes taste together.

KALE CAESAR SALAD

SERVES 8

PREP TIME 15 minutes

ADVANCE PREP Dressing may be made 2 days in advance; salad may be made 1 day in advance

EQUIPMENT Measuring cups and spoons • Garlic press • Cheese grater • Small bowl or 2-cup liquid measuring cup • Whisk • Cutting board • Knives • Tongs

Kale became trendy in the United States back in 2004 and is now popular both at home and in restaurants. My family started eating kale when my husband, Andy, who is *always* on a diet because of my work, met with a nutritionist who suggested that he add more leafy greens to his diet.

⅔ cup (165ml) mayonnaise

2 cloves garlic, crushed

Juice of ½ lemon

½ teaspoon Passover teriyaki or "soy" sauce (optional)

2 tablespoons water

Salt and black pepper

½ cup (50g) freshly grated Parmesan cheese, divided

1 bunch kale (8 ounces/225g), tough ribs removed

To prepare the dressing

IN A BOWL or 2-cup measuring cup, whisk together the mayonnaise, garlic, lemon juice, and teriyaki sauce, if using. Whisk in the water. Add salt and pepper to taste and half the Parmesan cheese and mix. May be made 1 day in advance; cover and store in the fridge.

To assemble the salad

STACK bunches of the kale leaves and slice them into ¼- to ½-inch-thick (6- to 12-mm) ribbons. Place into a large bowl. Add the dressing, a little at a time, tossing until all the leaves are coated with the dressing. Add the remaining cheese and more pepper to taste and toss.

GRATIN DAUPHINOIS

SERVES 8
PREP TIME 10 minutes
COOK TIME 50–60 minutes
ADVANCE PREP May be made 1 day in advance
EQUIPMENT Vegetable peeler • Cutting board •
Knives • Measuring cups and spoons • Cheese
grater • 8-inch (20-cm) square baking pan •
Large bowl • Silicone spatula

This is one of my favorite French recipes because
it combines potatoes and cream, baked with
cheese on top. When I spent three Passovers
in Geneva, Switzerland, I was always excited to
see the variety of kosher-for-Passover cheeses
that arrived in the kosher store from France and
Holland. If you find another strong-flavored hard
cheese, you can use that instead of the Parmesan.

1 tablespoon butter
1 clove garlic, peeled
3 large russet potatoes (2 pounds/1kg),
    peeled and thinly sliced into rounds
2 cups (480ml) heavy cream
1¼ teaspoons salt
Black or white pepper
2–3 tablespoons freshly grated Parmesan cheese

PREHEAT oven to 400°F (200°C).

RUB an 8-inch (20-cm) square baking pan with
a smidge of the 1 tablespoon butter—just enough
to coat the bottom and sides. Reserve remaining
butter.

RUB the garlic clove all around the pan and
discard.

PLACE the potato slices in a large bowl. Add the
cream, salt, and pepper to taste, using a silicone
spatula (or your hands) to toss and coat all the
potato slices. Layer the slices in the prepared pan
and pour any remaining cream over them. Cut the
remaining butter into pieces and scatter on top of
the potatoes. Sprinkle the cheese on top.

COVER and bake for 40 minutes, or until a
fork slides easily through the stack of potatoes.
Uncover and bake for another 10 minutes, or until
lightly browned on top. Let sit for 5 to 10 minutes
before serving to allow the potatoes to further
absorb the cream.

SEARED TUNA
WITH OLIVES AND CAPERS

SERVES 4-6
PREP TIME 10 minutes
COOK TIME 6–8 minutes
ADVANCE PREP May be made 1 day in advance
EQUIPMENT Measuring cups and spoons • Cutting board • Knives • Large frying pan • Silicone spatula

My family consumes a lot of sushi, so everyone is thrilled when I have seared tuna on the menu at our house. It is the quickest main dish to prepare if you, like my children, enjoy fresh tuna pretty raw; it cooks in minutes. The olive and caper relish has strong flavors, so I often serve it on the side. Several companies certify capers for Passover, but if you cannot find them, substitute green olives.

4 tuna steaks (6 ounces/170g each)
1/2 teaspoon dried basil
1/2 teaspoon dried thyme
Black pepper
3 tablespoons (45ml) extra virgin olive oil
3 tablespoons chopped red onion, cut into
    1/4-inch (6-mm) pieces
4 cloves garlic, chopped into 1/4-inch (6-mm)
    pieces
3 tablespoons capers, drained, or green olives,
    cut into 1/4-inch (6-mm) pieces
1/3 cup (45g) green or black olives
    (or a combination), cut into long slivers
1/2 teaspoon sugar

SPRINKLE both sides of the tuna steaks with the basil, thyme, and pepper to taste. Heat a large frying pan over high heat (do not add any oil). When the pan is hot, add the tuna steaks and cook for 1 to 1 1/2 minutes on each side, just long enough to sear the outside. Leave the center raw, unless you prefer tuna cooked all the way through.

REMOVE the tuna steaks to a plate. Reduce the heat to medium and add the oil. Add the red onion and garlic and cook for 2 minutes, stirring often. Add the capers, olives, sugar, and more pepper to taste and cook for 1 minute. Remove the pan from the heat.

PLACE the tuna steaks on a cutting board and slice into 1/3- to 1/2-inch-thick (8- to 12-mm) slices. Place the slices on a platter and sprinkle the caper and olive mixture on top, or serve it alongside in a small bowl.

RATATOUILLE

SERVES 8
PREP TIME 10 minutes
COOK TIME 20 minutes
ADVANCE PREP May be made 3 days in advance
EQUIPMENT Measuring cups and spoons • Cutting board • Knives • Medium saucepan • Wooden spoon or silicone spatula

Ratatouille is a Provençal vegetable stew that originated in the French city of Nice. There are many variations; sometimes I add a roughly chopped red pepper to the saucepan to cook with the eggplant. This dish may be served hot or cold as part of a meal or enjoyed as a snack, schmeared on matzoh.

2 tablespoons (30ml) extra virgin olive oil
1 onion, chopped into ½-inch (12-mm) pieces
1 large eggplant, not peeled, cut into 1-inch
   (2.5-cm) pieces
1 medium zucchini, not peeled, cut into ½-inch
   (12-mm) pieces
4 cloves garlic, roughly chopped
1 large fresh tomato, chopped into 1-inch (2.5-cm)
   pieces
1 tablespoon tomato sauce
¼ cup (60ml) water
6 fresh basil leaves, slivered, divided (see box,
   opposite)
Salt and black pepper

IN A MEDIUM SAUCEPAN, heat the oil over medium heat. Add the onion and cook for 3 minutes. Add the eggplant and cook, stirring often, for 5 minutes. Add the zucchini and cook for another 3 minutes. Add the garlic, tomato, tomato sauce, and water. Cover and cook for 10 minutes over low heat, or until the eggplant pieces are fork-tender. Season with salt and pepper to taste.

ADD two-thirds of the basil leaves, stir, and turn off the heat. When ready to serve, reheat the ratatouille and then sprinkle the remaining basil leaves on top.

SLIVERING BASIL

Stack the basil leaves and then roll up the long way. Cut across the roll to create thin slices. This is also called "chiffonade."

ITALIAN VEGETARIAN MENU

Although we have to live without pasta during Passover, there is no reason why we cannot enjoy other Italian favorites. This menu was inspired by trips to restaurants in Italy that featured enormous platters of roasted marinated vegetables and pillowlike gnocchi. It would also work as a lovely lunch.

This menu is a tribute to my father, Reubin Marcus, who served in Italy during World War II. In 1945, just prior to Passover, the Rochester Jewish Welfare Board shipped a massive amount of Passover essentials—matzoh, wine, gefilte fish—to the base where he was stationed in northern Italy. My father and his Jewish buddies decided to organize two Seders, but they needed more supplies, specifically additional food, dishes, utensils, tables, benches, and, most important, a large enough venue to host them.

The Jewish chaplain, without an official requisition, convinced the quartermaster to supply the required items, including new dishes and utensils, whereupon they filled up an entire truck with the supplies. My father and his buddies arranged to have the truck closely guarded to protect what was "taken" from black marketers. Searching the area, they found an old abandoned farm building that looked like it had not been used in a century. They cleaned it out, scraped down and painted the walls, and convened a Seder for three to four hundred Jewish soldiers. When word got out about how moving the first Seder was, even the top brass came to attend the second one, which surpassed the first, with upward of five hundred attendees. Following the holiday, the officers were so impressed with the cleanup job, they turned the building into an officers' club. My father says this story proves that with a little bit of dedication and moxie, you can turn nothing into something, and that it is truly possible to hold a Passover Seder anywhere.

MIXED VEGETABLE ANTIPASTI

SERVES 6
PREP TIME 10 minutes; roasted peppers need 25 minutes to cool before peeling
COOK TIME 30 minutes
ADVANCE PREP May be made 3 days in advance
EQUIPMENT Cutting board • Knives • Measuring spoons • Jelly roll or grill pan • Tongs • Medium bowl • Large platter

This platter is made with colorful bell peppers, portobello mushrooms, and fennel, but you can also grill eggplant, carrots, and zucchini slices. In addition to thyme leaves, you can sprinkle the top with slivered fresh basil leaves (see box on page 56). The mushrooms release a lot of liquid while cooking, so you need to cook them separately from the other vegetables.

2 red, yellow, or orange peppers, cut in half,
    seeds removed
1 large or 2 medium fennel bulbs, cut into
    1-inch-thick (2.5-cm) pieces
Extra virgin olive oil for drizzling
3 large portobello mushrooms
2 teaspoons balsamic vinegar, or more to taste
Salt and black pepper
Leaves of 3 thyme sprigs

PREHEAT oven to broil.

ON A JELLY ROLL OR GRILL PAN, arrange the
pepper halves, cut side down, and fennel pieces.
Drizzle enough oil over the vegetables so that
all the pieces are lightly coated. Roast on the
top rack for 15 minutes, or until the pepper skins
are almost all black and the fennel is just cooked
through. Check the fennel pieces after 10 to
12 minutes and remove to a plate any that are
already fork-tender.

WHEN THE PEPPERS ARE DONE, use tongs to
transfer them to a bowl and cover tightly with
plastic wrap. Let sit for 25 minutes or until cool.
Place the fennel pieces on a large plate or platter.
I like to arrange each type of vegetable in its own
vertical row on the platter. Place the mushrooms
on the pan, coat with some oil, and roast for 15
minutes, or until browned and fork-tender. Let
cool. Remove mushrooms from the pan and store
in a bowl in the fridge until ready to serve.

PEEL the skin off the peppers and discard. Cut
the peppers into 2-inch (5-cm) strips and place
on the platter. When ready to serve, cut the
mushrooms into ½-inch-thick (12-mm) slices and
place on the platter. Drizzle all of the vegetables
with olive oil and balsamic vinegar to taste,
sprinkle with black pepper, and scatter the thyme
leaves on top. Serve at room temperature.

PAN-SEARED ZUCCHINI WITH GARLIC

SERVES 6
PREP TIME 10 minutes
COOK TIME 10–12 minutes
ADVANCE PREP May be made 2 days in advance
EQUIPMENT Cutting board • Knives • Measuring
spoons • Large frying pan • Silicone spatula •
Garlic press

The key to making these zucchini sticks crisp and
not mushy is to cook them in a hot pan in batches.
If you crowd the pan, it takes longer for the pieces
to brown because they start to release moisture.

3 teaspoons extra virgin olive oil, divided
4 large zucchini, not peeled, cut into
    1½-inch-thick (4-cm) pieces, divided
2 cloves garlic, crushed, divided
¼ teaspoon salt, divided

HEAT 2 teaspoons of the oil in a large frying pan
over medium-high heat. When hot, add half the
zucchini pieces and let sit without stirring until
they start to brown on the bottom. Stir and cook
for another 2 minutes so that the other sides
brown. Stir again. Cook until browned on all
sides and fork-tender but not too soft, stirring
occasionally. Stir in half the crushed garlic and
cook for 1 minute, stirring often. Add ⅛ teaspoon
of the salt and stir. Transfer to a serving bowl.

RETURN the pan to the stovetop and heat for
30 seconds. Add the remaining zucchini. Let sit
untouched for a minute or two and then stir. If
the pan is no longer shiny, add the remaining
teaspoon oil and stir. Cook until the zucchini is
browned on all sides, and then add the remaining
garlic and ⅛ teaspoon salt and cook for another
minute. Stir into the first batch and serve warm.

EGGPLANT PARMESAN

SERVES 12–15
PREP TIME 10 minutes
COOK TIME 20 minutes to fry eggplant;
35–40 minutes to bake
ADVANCE PREP May be assembled 1 day in
advance, fully baked 3 days in advance, or frozen;
thaw completely before reheating
EQUIPMENT Cutting board • Knives • Measuring
cups and spoons • 2 shallow bowls • Large frying
pan • 9 x 13-inch (23 x 33-cm) baking pan •
Silicone spatula

Eggplant Parmesan is one of my favorite Italian
dishes. It is best made by my brother Adam
Marcus, who has paid his rent for occasionally
living with us by lovingly making his master
version of this dish with a homemade sauce.
Although I try to avoid frying foods (except for
doughnuts and chicken once a year), I find that
eggplant Parmesan tastes better made with
breaded and fried eggplant slices. If desired, you
can grill the slices in the oven until fork-tender
and then layer and bake as described below. If
you go the healthier route, sprinkle the oven-
roasted slices with some garlic powder, salt,
and black pepper. Depending on the size of the
eggplants, you will end up with two or three
layers in the pan.

1/3–1/2 cup (80–120ml) oil for frying
3 large eggs, beaten
1 1/2 cups (210g) Passover breadcrumbs or
   matzoh meal (200g)
1/2 teaspoon garlic powder
1 1/2 teaspoons dried oregano
Salt and black pepper
2 medium eggplants, not peeled, sliced into
   3/4-inch-thick (2-cm) rounds

1 1/2–2 cups (360–480 ml) tomato sauce
2 cups (240g) shredded mozzarella cheese, or
   more as needed
1/3 cup (35g) freshly grated Parmesan cheese

PREHEAT oven to 350°F (180°C).

PLACE a large frying pan on the stovetop and
add 1/3 cup (80ml) oil. Pour the beaten eggs into
a shallow bowl. In another bowl, stir together
the breadcrumbs, garlic powder, and oregano
and season with salt and pepper to taste. Heat
the oil over medium-high heat. When the oil is
hot, fry the eggplant slices in batches, browning
both sides, until fork-tender, about 10 minutes
per batch. Transfer to a plate covered with paper
towels. Add more oil to the pan between batches
if the pan gets dry.

USING a silicone spatula, spread about 3/4 cup
(180ml) of the tomato sauce in the bottom of a
9 x 13-inch (23 x 33-cm) baking pan. Place one
layer of eggplant slices on top. Sprinkle with 1 cup
of the shredded cheese. Cover with a second
layer of eggplant. Pour another 3/4 cup (180ml)
sauce on top and use the spatula to spread the
sauce on top of the eggplant pieces. Sprinkle with
1 cup (120g) of the shredded cheese. If you have
more eggplant slices, place them on top, then add
some tomato sauce and more shredded cheese.
Sprinkle the Parmesan all over the top.

COVER the pan tightly with aluminum foil and
bake for 35 to 40 minutes, or until the eggplant
layers are heated through and the cheese is
melted. If you assembled the dish in advance and
stored it in the fridge but did not bake it, bake for
an extra 20 minutes.

Until I developed this recipe, homemade gnocchi were never good to me. I had enjoyed gnocchi prepared by Italian chefs, but the few times I tried making them myself, the gnocchi dissolved in the boiling water. These, however, came out perfectly. You can serve them with the sauce featured here, as well as with a variety of alternatives, such as a few tablespoons of melted butter and fresh chopped sage leaves; simply with olive oil and grated cheese; or with pesto (for recipe, see box opposite, page 65). It does take time to roll and shape gnocchi, so find some helpers.

1½ teaspoons kosher salt
3 large russet potatoes
   (about 2½ pounds/1360g)
¾ cup (120g) potato starch, plus extra
   for dusting
1 large egg
1 tablespoon extra virgin olive oil
1 teaspoon salt, plus more for salting
   cooking water
Black pepper
1 cup (240ml) tomato sauce
⅓ cup (80ml) light cream
⅓ cup (35g) freshly grated Parmesan cheese

POTATO GNOCCHI WITH PINK SAUCE

SERVES 8

PREP TIME 10 minutes to make dough and 30 minutes to chill it; 25 minutes to roll and shape gnocchi

COOK TIME 30 minutes to cook potatoes; 20 minutes to boil gnocchi in batches; 3 minutes to cook sauce

ADVANCE PREP Dough or cooked gnocchi may be made 1 day in advance

EQUIPMENT Measuring cups and spoons • Cutting board • Knives • Medium saucepan • Colander • Medium bowl • Potato masher • Wooden spoon • Large saucepan • Small saucepan

To prepare the potatoes

BRING a medium saucepan of water to a boil and add the kosher salt. Scrub the skins of the potatoes and cut in half; leave the peels on. Boil the potatoes until fork-tender, about 30 minutes. Drain the potatoes and return them to the saucepan; turn the heat to low and let the potatoes sit for 2 to 3 minutes, stirring once or twice, to dry them out.

To make the dough

LET the potatoes cool just until you can peel them; the skin should come off easily. Place the peeled potatoes in a medium bowl and mash them really well. Add the potato starch, egg, oil, salt, and pepper to taste, and mix well. Dump the dough onto the counter and knead for a few minutes. Place the dough in a bowl, cover with plastic wrap, and store in the fridge for 30 minutes.

To make the gnocchi

BRING a large saucepan of water to a boil and add some salt. Divide the dough into six equal parts. Dust your hands with a little potato starch and roll each piece into a 1-inch-thick (2.5-cm) snake. Cut each snake into ¾-inch (2-cm) pieces and roll each piece into an oblong ball. Press each ball into the tines of a fork to make lines.

ADD the gnocchi to the boiling water in batches (each snake equals 1 batch) without crowding the pan. They will sink to the bottom of the pan. Once they bob to the surface, cook for 1 minute. Drain the cooked gnocchi in a colander and pour them into a serving dish.

To prepare the pink sauce

PLACE the tomato sauce in a small saucepan over medium heat. When the sauce starts to bubble, add the cream and stir. Turn the heat to low and cook until heated through, about 2 minutes. Ladle the sauce over the gnocchi, and add some black pepper and the Parmesan cheese.

PESTO SAUCE

SERVES 8
PREP TIME 5 minutes
ADVANCE PREP May be made 3 days in advance
EQUIPMENT Measuring cups and spoons • Knives • Cheese grater • Food processsor • Silicone spatula

3 cloves garlic, crushed
2 tablespoons pine nuts
1½ cups fresh basil leaves
½ cup (50g) freshly grated Parmesan cheese
¾ cup (180ml) extra virgin olive oil
Salt and black pepper

PLACE the garlic and pine nuts in the bowl of a food processor and process until finely ground. Add the basil leaves and process until the basil is chopped into very tiny pieces. Add the Parmesan cheese and process again. Scrape down the bowl with a silicone spatula and process again for a few seconds. While the machine is running, pour the olive oil in slowly until it is all mixed into the pesto. Season with salt and pepper to taste. Store in the fridge for up to 4 days.

BBQ DINNER MENU

The holiday of Passover has several names, including Chag Ha'Aviv, the holiday of spring. In Maryland, where I live, Passover usually coincides with the weather getting warmer, and we start to eat on our covered porch. A Passover barbeque is the perfect way to celebrate spring and enjoy a casual dinner during a holiday that includes a multitude of formal meals. Of course, if it remains cold where you are, you can always cook the steak indoors.

SHREDDED BRUSSELS SPROUTS SALAD

SERVES 6–8
PREP TIME 20 minutes
ADVANCE PREP May be made 1 day in advance
EQUIPMENT Cutting board • Knives • Cookie sheet
• Measuring cups and spoons • Small bowl • Whisk

At every family meal, I make sure to serve some raw vegetables in addition to the cooked ones. You will be surprised by how much you like this crunchy salad of raw Brussels sprouts.

1 pound (450g) Brussels sprouts (preferably
   larger-size ones), ends trimmed,
   2 outer layers of leaves removed
¾ cup (115g) whole almonds, toasted
   (see box, page 34)
½ small red onion, chopped into small pieces
   (about ¼ cup/40g)
3 tablespoons (45ml) fresh lemon juice
   (from 1 lemon)
¼ cup (60ml) extra virgin olive oil
1 tablespoon honey
⅛ teaspoon salt
⅛ teaspoon black pepper

CUT the Brussels sprouts in half the long way, from the stem end to the top, and thinly slice. Place the sliced sprouts in a bowl. Roughly chop the toasted almonds and add to the bowl, along with the chopped onion. In a small bowl, whisk together the lemon juice, oil, honey, salt, and black pepper. Pour the dressing over the salad and toss.

WASHING SHREDDED BRUSSELS SPROUTS

You should follow your own rabbinic authority for instructions on cleaning and inspecting Brussels sprouts. For this recipe, I trim off the ends and then remove and discard two layers of the outer leaves. I rinse the sprouts and then slice them. To be extra careful about eliminating bugs, soak the shredded sprouts in water, drain them, and check the water. If you see any dirt or bugs, repeat the process. Make sure the sprouts are dry before making this salad.

12 (3-inch/7.5-cm) round new potatoes,
   or 2½ pounds (1.2kg) small round potatoes,
   not peeled
1½ teaspoons kosher salt, plus more to taste
4 tablespoons (60ml) extra virgin olive oil, divided
4 cloves crushed garlic
Black pepper

HALF FILL a medium saucepan with water, bring
to a boil over high heat, and add 1 teaspoon salt.
Add the potatoes and cook until you can just
pierce them with a fork, 20 to 25 minutes. Drain,
let cool, and dry completely. May be made 2 days
in advance and stored in the fridge.

PREHEAT oven to 450°F (230°C).

LINE a jelly roll pan with aluminum foil or use a
roasting pan. Drizzle with 1 tablespoon of the oil
and rub to coat. Add the cooled potatoes to the
pan, place paper towels or a dish towel on top,
and press down on each potato to flatten it until it
is about 1-inch (2.5-cm) thick. (If you refrigerated
the potatoes overnight, first warm them in the
microwave so they are easier to smash.)

DRIZZLE the potatoes with the remaining
3 tablespoons (45ml) oil, making sure that they
are all well oiled. Sprinkle the potatoes with the
crushed garlic, the remaining ½ teaspoon salt
or more to taste, and pepper to taste. Roast for
30 minutes, or until crispy.

SMASHED POTATOES

SERVES 6
PREP TIME 15 minutes
COOK TIME 20–25 minutes to cook potatoes,
30 minutes to roast them
ADVANCE PREP Potatoes may be boiled 2 days in
advance, but taste best when roasted just before
serving
EQUIPMENT Medium saucepan • Garlic press •
Measuring cups and spoons • Colander • Jelly roll
pan or roasting pan

These small potatoes are boiled and then literally
smashed—pressed down and partially flattened—
and then roasted in the oven. The result is potatoes
with a soft interior and crispy exterior.

GARLIC-MARINATED STEAK WITH ONION JAM

SERVES 6
PREP TIME 15 minutes
COOK TIME 35 minutes for jam; 16 minutes for steak
ADVANCE PREP Onions may be made 3 days in advance; meat must be marinated for 2 hours or overnight; meat may be grilled 1 day in advance
EQUIPMENT Measuring cups and spoons • Cutting board • Knives • Large container or 1-gallon (3.7-L) freezer bag • Garlic press • Medium saucepan • Wooden spoon

It is a good idea to fully clean and *kasher* your outdoor grill for Passover, because grilling is a great way to serve a crowd without a lot of effort. Although every year, more and more companies come out with sauces and condiments that are kosher for Passover, it is always healthier to make your own. This onion jam is easy to prepare in advance and possesses a tasty balance of tart and sweet, which you can adjust by adding a little more sugar or vinegar, as you like. You can serve the jam with any cut of steak.

FOR THE MARINADE

8 cloves garlic, crushed
¼–½ teaspoon black pepper to taste
¼ cup (60ml) extra virgin olive oil
⅓ cup (80ml) white wine
3 pounds (1.5kg) London broil

FOR THE ONION JAM

¼ cup (60ml) extra virgin olive oil
3 medium onions, halved and thinly sliced
   (about 4 cups/640g)
3 tablespoons (40g) light brown sugar
1 teaspoon apple cider vinegar
Salt and black pepper

To make the marinade
PLACE the garlic, pepper, oil and wine in a container or 1-gallon (3.7-L) freezer bag. Shake or stir to mix. Add the meat and cover or seal. Let marinate for 2 hours or overnight.

To make the onion jam
HEAT the oil in a medium saucepan, add the onions, and cook over medium to medium-high heat for 15 minutes, stirring often, until the onions are very browned. Add the sugar and cook on low heat, uncovered, for 20 minutes, or until the onions are caramelized and most of the sugar has melted and been absorbed. Stir occasionally.

REMOVE from the heat, add the vinegar, season with salt and pepper, and let cool. May be made 3 days in advance; store, covered, in the fridge. Serve the jam warm or at room temperature.

To prepare the steak
PREHEAT broiler or outdoor grill.

BROIL or grill the meat for 8 to 10 minutes per side. The cooking time will depend on the cut and whether you like rare or medium-cooked meat. Let the meat sit for 5 minutes and then slice against the grain. Serve with the onion jam.

ROASTED EGGPLANT WITH BELL PEPPER VINAIGRETTE

SERVES 6-8
PREP TIME 10 minutes
COOK TIME 17 minutes
ADVANCE PREP May be made 2 days in advance; finished dish needs to marinate for 2 hours
EQUIPMENT Cutting board • Knives • Measuring spoons • Pastry brush • Grill or baking pan • Medium frying pan • Tongs • Silicone spatula

This a tasty room-temperature side dish that you should make in advance, along with the onion jam on page 71, so that when you are ready to grill, most of your meal is already prepared. I broil the eggplant slices in the oven, but you also can cook them on the grill before you cook the steak.

2 medium eggplants, not peeled, cut into
   ¾-inch-thick (2-cm) slices
5 tablespoons (75ml) extra virgin olive oil
Ground cumin and turmeric for dusting eggplant
½ red pepper, seeded and cut into ¼-inch
   (6-mm) cubes
½ yellow pepper, seeded and cut
   into ¼-inch (6-mm) cubes
½ medium red onion, finely chopped
2 tablespoons sugar
3 tablespoons white or apple cider vinegar
Salt and black pepper

To prepare the eggplant
PREHEAT broiler.

POUR 1 tablespoon of the oil on a grill pan or other baking pan and rub to coat. Add the eggplant slices in one layer and brush with another tablespoon of oil. Sprinkle a little cumin and turmeric on top. Broil for 5 to 7 minutes, or until browned. Turn over the eggplant slices, sprinkle with some more cumin and turmeric, and add some black pepper. Broil for another 4 to 5 minutes. Let cool for 3 minutes and then transfer to a serving platter.

To prepare the peppers and onions
HEAT 3 tablespoons (45ml) of the oil in a medium frying pan over medium-high heat. Add the diced red and yellow peppers and onions and cook for 3 minutes. Add the sugar, vinegar, salt, and pepper to taste and cook for 1 minute.

TO ASSEMBLE the dish, scatter the pepper and onion mixture over the eggplant slices, making sure to place some on top of all the slices as well as under them. Let the dish marinate for 2 hours or overnight. Serve at room temperature.

CUTTING PEPPERS

To cut bell peppers into small dice (cubes), first cut the peppers in half, from the stem end to the bottom, and remove the seeds and white pith. Cut in half again lengthwise. Slice each part the long way into ¼-inch-thick (6-mm) slices. Gather the slices together and cut them across into small cubes. Repeat with the other pepper quarters.

EASY CHICKEN MENU

This is a simple weekday menu that you can put on the table within 45 minutes; just be sure to cook the quinoa earlier in the day, so that it can cool. When you are ready to make dinner, roast the sweet potatoes for the quinoa first, place the carrots in the oven, and then start the chicken. While everything cooks and or stays warm, prepare the Greek salad.

GREEK SALAD

SERVES 6–8

PREP TIME 15 minutes

ADVANCE PREP Dressing may be made 3 days in advance; salad ingredients, minus the avocado, may be tossed earlier in the day.

EQUIPMENT Cutting board • Knives • Measuring cups and spoons • Large bowl • Small bowl • Whisk • Garlic press

FOR THE SALAD

1 scallion, chopped into 1/2-inch (12-mm) pieces

1/2 green or red pepper, chopped into 3/4-inch (2-cm) pieces

8 pitted green olives, halved or quartered the long way

1 stalk celery, cut into 3/4-inch (2-cm) pieces

1/2 small red onion, chopped into 1/4-inch (6-mm) pieces

1/2 English (hothouse) cucumber, not peeled, chopped into 1-inch (2.5-cm) pieces

1 avocado, pitted, peeled, and cubed (optional)

2 handfuls spinach or watercress leaves

3/4 cup cherry tomatoes, cut in half

5 fresh basil leaves, slivered (see box, page 56)

FOR THE DRESSING

Juice of 1/2 lemon (about 1 1/2 tablespoons)

1/4 cup (60ml) extra virgin olive oil

1/2 teaspoon dried oregano or thyme

1 garlic clove, crushed

Salt and black pepper

To make the salad

IN A LARGE BOWL, place the scallion, bell pepper, olives, celery, red onion, cucumber, avocado, spinach, cherry tomatoes, and basil and toss. If you prepare the salad earlier in the day, wait until just before serving to add the avocado.

To make the dressing

IN A SMALL BOWL, whisk together the lemon juice, oil, oregano, garlic, and salt and pepper to taste.

POUR the dressing over the salad and toss.

ROASTED PEPPERED CARROTS

SERVES 6

PREP TIME 5 minutes

COOK TIME 25 minutes

ADVANCE PREP May be made 2 days in advance

EQUIPMENT Vegetable peeler • Measuring spoons • Cutting board • Knives • Jelly roll or roasting pan

I first tasted these peppery carrots at my friend Kathy Ingber's Shabbat table. You will need to roast them just until they are cooked through, so that they don't get too soft.

12 large carrots, peeled, ends trimmed

1 1/2 tablespoons (22ml) extra virgin olive oil

1/4 teaspoon black pepper, or more to taste

Salt

PREHEAT oven to 400°F (200°C). Line a jelly roll pan with foil or use a roasting pan.

SLICE the carrots crosswise into thirds. If the carrots are thick, cut them in half or quarters to make 1/2 x 3-inch (1.2 x 7.5-cm) sticks. Make sure that all the pieces are about the same thickness. Place the carrots in the pan, add the oil and pepper, and toss to coat. Roast the carrots for 25 minutes, stirring once or twice, until you can just pierce them with a fork. Remove the carrots from the oven, add salt to taste, and toss. Serve warm or at room temperature.

CRUNCHY QUINOA WITH SWEET POTATOES AND CRANBERRIES

SERVES 6-8

PREP TIME 10 minutes; 30 minutes for quinoa to cool

COOK TIME 30 minutes

ADVANCE PREP Quinoa may be cooked or salad assembled 2 days in advance

EQUIPMENT Measuring cups and spoons • Cutting board • Knives • Small saucepan • Roasting pan • Spatula • Small frying pan • Small bowl • Whisk • Large bowl

Quinoa is the greatest new addition to the Passover pantry. It finally received definitive rabbinic approval for Passover in 2014, after a rabbi was dispatched to Peru and Bolivia to see how quinoa is grown. He learned that quinoa grows at very high altitudes, while the grains that are prohibited on Passover are grown much farther below it. The authorities concluded that there was no risk of intermingling. My husband, Andy, eats quinoa for breakfast with blueberries all Passover long. This dish is a great combination of color and texture.

1 cup (170g) quinoa

2 cups (480ml) water

1 medium sweet potato, peeled and cut into ½-inch (12-mm) cubes

4 tablespoons (60ml) extra virgin olive oil, divided

2 teaspoons apple cider vinegar

1 teaspoon honey

½ teaspoon ground cumin

¼ teaspoon ground cinnamon

¼ teaspoon salt

¼ teaspoon black pepper

⅓ cup (45g) pine nuts, toasted (see box, page 2)

⅓ cup (45g) dried cranberries

3 scallions, cut into ¼-inch-thick (6-mm) slices

PREHEAT oven to 400°F.

To prepare the quinoa
PLACE quinoa in a small saucepan with the water. Bring to a boil and then reduce heat and simmer, covered, for 15 minutes, or until the water has evaporated. Turn off the heat and let the quinoa sit, covered, for at least half an hour. The quinoa may be cooked 2 days in advance and stored covered in the fridge.

PLACE the sweet potato cubes in a roasting pan and toss with 1 tablespoon of the oil. Roast for 25 minutes, or until the cubes can be pierced with a fork. Set aside.

To prepare the dressing
IN A SMALL BOWL, whisk together the remaining 3 tablespoons (45ml) oil with the vinegar, honey, cumin, cinnamon, salt, and pepper.

To assemble the dish
USE a whisk to break apart any clumps of quinoa that may have formed as it cooled and transfer it to a large bowl. Add the dressing and whisk well. Add the sweet potatoes, pine nuts, cranberries, and scallions and mix gently. Serve at room temperature.

ABOVE: *Roasted Peppered Carrots,
page 77*; BELOW: *Crunchy
Quinoa with Sweet Potatoes and
Cranberries, opposite.*

CHICKEN SCALOPPINI WITH MUSHROOMS

SERVES 6–8
PREP TIME 20 minutes
COOK TIME 25 minutes
ADVANCE PREP May be made 2 days in advance
EQUIPMENT Measuring cups and spoons • Cutting board • Knives • 1-gallon (3.7-L) freezer bag • Large frying pan with 2-inch sides • 9 x 13-inch (23 x 33-cm) roasting pan

I was thrilled when my local kosher butcher started selling boneless chicken already cut into really thin slices—because the slices cook in minutes. See box, page 44 for instructions how to slice thick boneless breasts.

⅓ cup (80ml) extra virgin olive oil
½ cup (80g) potato starch or matzoh
   cake meal (65g)
¼ teaspoon salt, plus more to taste
½ teaspoon black pepper, plus more to taste
8–10 chicken scaloppini or boneless chicken
   breasts, thinly sliced or pounded
   (see box, page 44)

CLEANING MUSHROOMS

For years we were cautioned against fully washing mushrooms because they could absorb too much water. The best way to clean mushrooms is to rinse them under a light stream of water and then wipe off any dirt. Dry well and wipe or rinse off. Now experts recommend this method, too.

8 shiitake mushrooms, cleaned and cut into
   ⅓- to ½-inch-thick (8- to 12-mm) slices
8 button mushrooms, cleaned and sliced into
   ⅓- to ½-inch-thick (8- to12-mm) slices
½ cup (120ml) white wine
½ teaspoon fresh or dried thyme leaves
2 cups (500ml) chicken or vegetable broth
3 tablespoons (45ml) fresh lemon juice
   (from 1 lemon)
2 teaspoons finely chopped fresh parsley leaves
   for garnish

To prepare the chicken
PREHEAT oven to 250°F.

HEAT the oil in a large frying pan over medium-high heat. Place the potato starch, salt, and pepper in a large plastic bag and shake to mix. Add the chicken breasts, three at a time, close the bag, and shake to coat. Shake off the excess. Add the breasts to the frying pan and cook for 2 to 4 minutes per side, or until you see some browned parts. Transfer the cooked chicken to a 9 x 13-inch (23 x 33-cm) roasting pan. Repeat with the rest of the chicken and keep it warm in the oven.

To prepare the sauce
ADD the mushrooms to the same frying pan and cook for 2 minutes, stirring often. Add the wine and thyme and cook for 2 minutes more, or until the wine starts to evaporate. Add the broth and lemon juice and cook for another 2 to 3 minutes, or until the sauce thickens a little.

To assemble the dish
REMOVE the chicken from the oven. Pour the sauce over the chicken, turning the breasts to coat both sides. Add salt and black pepper to taste and sprinkle with the chopped parsley. Serve immediately or place into the oven to keep warm until serving.

BREAKFAST

We are told that breakfast is the most important meal of the day, but when it comes to breakfast on Passover, we would rather just sleep through it, as my kids often do. No toast, no bagels, no decent breakfast cereals, and no oatmeal add up to a grumpy family. One year, I remember making omelets for everyone day after day. This chapter is my way of giving you and your family healthy and tasty morning or lunchtime options.

FRITTATA WITH BROCCOLI AND LEEKS

SERVES 4–6
PREP TIME 10 minutes
COOK TIME 33–35 minutes
ADVANCE PREP May be made 2 days in advance
EQUIPMENT Cutting board • Knives • Garlic press • Measuring cups and spoons • Large ovenproof frying pan with 2-inch (5-cm) sides and a cover • Large bowl • Whisk • Silicone spatula

Unlike traditional omelets, which can be tricky to prepare, a frittata is a baked vegetable omelet that requires no special skills. I have served this frittata for breakfast, lunch, and even as a light dinner with home-fried potatoes.

3 tablespoons (45ml) extra virgin olive oil
2 leeks, white and light green parts only, cut into ⅓-inch-thick (8-mm) slices
2 cloves garlic, crushed
1 head broccoli, chopped into 1-inch pieces (about 2 cups/180g)
2 tablespoons water
10 large eggs
½ cup (120ml) milk (any kind)
Salt and black pepper
½ cup (30g) shredded Cheddar cheese

PREHEAT oven to 350°F (180°C).

HEAT 2 tablespoons of the oil in a large frying pan with 2-inch (5-cm) sides over medium-low heat. Add the leeks and garlic and cook for 5 minutes, or until the leeks are translucent. Add the broccoli and cook over medium-low heat for 5 minutes. Add the water, stir, and then cover and cook for another 3 to 5 minutes, or until the broccoli is almost fork-tender. Add the remaining tablespoon oil and stir.

IN A LARGE BOWL, whisk together the eggs, milk, and salt and pepper to taste. Pour into the pan and cook without stirring over medium-low heat until the edges start to set, about 3 minutes. Sprinkle the cheese on top. Place the pan in the oven (do not cover) and bake for 15 to 17 minutes, or until set.

RUN a silicone spatula around the edges of the pan and flip the frittata onto a plate, or scoop out slices. Serve warm.

GLUTEN-FREE WAFFLES OR PANCAKES
{ gluten-free }

MAKES 4 LARGE WAFFLES OR 6-8 MEDIUM PANCAKES

PREP TIME 10 minutes

COOK TIME 15 minutes

ADVANCE PREP Batter may be made 1 day in advance; waffles may be made 1 day in advance and reheated

EQUIPMENT Measuring cups and spoons • Zester • Medium bowl • Electric mixer • Whisk • Waffle maker • Silicone spatula

In 2013, my family was in Israel for Passover, so I won the get-out-of-Passover-cooking-free card that year. The hotels in Israel serve enormous breakfast buffets with every kind of salad, cheese, yogurt, fruit, cake, bread (for Passover—really), and cookie you can imagine. I was fascinated by the appearance of waffles at two different hotel buffets, and my kids were thrilled. One hotel even had a frozen yogurt machine—the yogurt made an excellent topping. After tasting the waffles, I was won over and convinced that everyone needs a waffle maker for Passover. This batter can be used to make pancakes as well.

1¼ cups (150g) ground almonds
1 teaspoon Passover baking powder
¼ cup (50g) sugar
2 tablespoons vanilla sugar (see box, page 98)
½ cup (80g) potato starch
2 large eggs, separated
½ cup (120ml) milk
½ teaspoon orange zest (from 1 orange)
½ teaspoon salt
Nonstick cooking spray

IN A MEDIUM BOWL, whisk together the ground almonds, baking powder, sugar, vanilla sugar, and potato starch. Add the egg yolks and whisk. Add the milk and orange zest and whisk to combine.

IN A LARGE BOWL or the bowl of a stand mixer, beat the egg whites at medium speed and, when the eggs are foamy, add the salt. Turn the speed up to high and beat the whites until stiff. Gently fold the egg whites into the batter.

HEAT your waffle maker and generously coat it with cooking spray.

MEASURE about ¾ cup (180ml) of batter for an average waffle maker. Drop batter in the middle of the waffle maker. Slowly close the top. Let the waffle cook for about 4 minutes, or until browned. Remove from waffle maker and serve.

BEATING EGG WHITES

Before beating, egg whites should be at room temperature, or at least be removed from the fridge an hour beforehand. To warm quickly, place whites in a bowl over another bowl filled with 2 inches (5cm) hot water for 10 minutes. Whip the egg whites on medium speed until foamy, and then reduce the speed to low and add a pinch of salt or few drops of lemon juice. Return the speed to medium for a few seconds and then increase it to high. Soft peaks bend slightly when you lift up the whisk or beater. For stiff peaks, beat until the peak stands straight up when you lift the beaters.

FRUIT AND NUT GRANOLA
{ gluten-free }

MAKES 8 ½ CUPS
PREP TIME 5–10 minutes
COOK TIME 45–50 minutes
ADVANCE PREP May be made 1 week in advance
EQUIPMENT Measuring cups and spoons • Jelly roll or large roasting pan • Large bowl • Silicone spatula • Liquid measuring cup or microwave-safe bowl • Cutting board • Knives • 1-gallon (3.7-L) freezer bag or airtight container

I love the Passover granola recipe that I premiered on my blog, thekosherbaker.com, and published in *The Holiday Kosher Baker*. It includes whole-wheat matzoh farfel (½-inch/12-mm or smaller matzoh pieces), which gives the granola a terrific crunch. This time I created a granola that is all natural and gluten-free. My family loves it so much that they want it in the house all the time. We eat it in yogurt, as a cereal with milk, and as a snack.

1½ cups (128g) dried coconut flakes
1½ cups (180g) pecan halves, chopped into
 ½-inch (12-mm) pieces
1 cup (120g) cashews, chopped into ½-inch
 (12-mm) pieces
¾ cup (90g) walnut halves, chopped into ½-inch
 (12-mm) pieces
¾ cup (115g) whole almonds, chopped into
 ½-inch (12-mm) pieces
1 teaspoon ground cinnamon
½ teaspoon salt
¾ cup (180ml) maple syrup or honey
3 tablespoons (45ml) vegetable oil
4 teaspoons light brown sugar
¾ cup (100g) dried cranberries
½ cup (80g) raisins
¾ cup (120g) chopped dates or dried apricots
 (no larger than ½-inch (12-mm) pieces)

PREHEAT oven to 300°F (150°C).

LINE a jelly roll pan with parchment paper, making sure the paper goes ½ inch (12 mm) up the sides of the pan, or use a roasting pan. Place the coconut, pecans, cashews, walnuts, almonds, cinnamon, and salt in the pan and toss.

IN A 1-CUP LIQUID MEASURING CUP or microwave-safe bowl, combine the maple syrup, oil, and brown sugar; heat in the microwave oven for 45 seconds, or until the sugar dissolves. Stir well. Pour the syrup over the nut mixture and toss to coat.

SPREAD the nut mixture evenly on the prepared baking pan and bake for 45 to 50 minutes, stirring every 10 minutes, until the nuts are browned. Let cool in the pan for 30 minutes. Mix in the dried cranberries, raisins, and dates. May be made up to 1 week ahead; store in a freezer bag or airtight container.

VARIATIONS

- For vanilla flavor, add 1 teaspoon vanilla or 2 teaspoons vanilla sugar to the maple, oil, and sugar mixture.

- Substitute pistachios or hazelnuts for any of the nuts.

- Substitute any dried fruit, such as plums, mangoes, or figs.

CRUMB CAKE MUFFINS
{ gluten-free }

MAKES 16–18 MUFFINS

PREP TIME 15 minutes; let butter sit for 15 minutes to soften

COOK TIME 22–25 minutes

ADVANCE PREP May be made 3 days in advance or frozen

EQUIPMENT Two muffin tins and paper liners (can be disposable) • Electric mixer • 2 large mixing bowls • Measuring cups and spoons • Silicone spatula • Cutting board • Knives • Medium bowl

These muffins have a scrumptious crunchy top and a soft cakey interior. You can make these parve by substituting water and margarine for the milk and butter.

FOR THE BATTER

4 large eggs, separated
½ cup (100g) sugar
½ cup (110g) packed light brown sugar
2 teaspoons vanilla (optional)
¼ cup (60ml) milk
¾ cup (90g) gluten-free cake meal or potato starch (120g)
Dash salt

FOR THE STREUSEL TOPPING

1 tablespoon ground cinnamon
½ cup (110g) packed light brown sugar
½ cup (60g) pecan halves, chopped into ⅓-inch (8-mm) pieces
½ cup (60g) walnut halves, chopped into ⅓-inch (8-mm) pieces
3 tablespoons (42g) unsalted butter, at room temperature
1 tablespoon gluten-free cake meal or potato starch

PREHEAT oven to 350°F (180°C).

PLACE paper cups into 16 to 18 cups of two muffin tins.

To make the batter
PLACE the yolks, sugar, brown sugar, vanilla, if using, and milk in a medium bowl and beat with an electric mixer at medium speed for 1 minute. Add the cake meal and beat for 2 minutes more until mixed. Set aside.

IN A SEPARATE BOWL, beat the egg whites on low speed until foamy. Add the salt, and then beat the egg whites on high speed until stiff. Use a silicone spatula to fold the whites into the batter in four parts, mixing at increasingly slower speeds after each addition until all the whites are incorporated.

To make the streusel
IN A MEDIUM BOWL, mix the cinnamon, brown sugar, pecans, and walnuts. Add the butter and cake meal and use your fingers to work the mixture until it sticks together. When the mixture comes together, break it back into crumbs.

FILL the muffin cups two-thirds to three-fourths full with the batter. Sprinkle the crumbs on top, dividing them evenly among the muffins.

BAKE for 22 to 25 minutes, or until a toothpick inserted into the center of a muffin comes out clean. Serve warm or at room temperature.

PASSOVER ROLLS
[gebrokts • nut-free }

MAKES 8 ROLLS

PREP TIME 10 minutes; let batter sit for 1 hour before baking

BAKE TIME 60 minutes

ADVANCE PREP May be made 2 days in advance or frozen

EQUIPMENT Measuring cups and spoons • Medium saucepan • Large bowl • Wooden spoon • Cookie sheet

My assistant, Diana Ash, and I tested this recipe more than any other because we were never satisfied with the outcome. I like cutting the rolls in half, toasting them in the oven, and then slathering them with butter. Think tuna melts or grilled cheese sandwiches, or fill them with cream cheese, smoked salmon, and avocado. The possibilities are endless.

1⅓ cups (320ml) water

⅔ cup (160ml) vegetable oil

2 tablespoons sugar

2 teaspoons salt

½ teaspoon black pepper

2 cups plus 2 tablespoons (293g) matzoh
  cake meal

6 large eggs

PREHEAT oven to 350°F (180°C).

IN A MEDIUM SAUCEPAN over medium-high heat, bring the water, oil, sugar, salt, and pepper to a boil. Stir to dissolve the sugar. Remove from the heat, add the cake meal, and use a wooden spoon to mix. Transfer to a large bowl. Add the eggs, one at a time, mixing well after each addition. You can use a hand-held electric mixer for this if you like. Let batter sit at room temperature, covered, for 1 hour.

LINE a cookie sheet with parchment paper. Divide the batter into eight equal portions and, using wet hands, shape into oval or round rolls. Bake for 60 minutes, or until golden brown.

ABOVE: *Triple-Chocolate Biscotti, page 94;*
BELOW: *Fully Loaded Cookie Bars, page 98.*

DESSERTS

Passover is the holiday when you *have* to be a home baker. Even major cities have few bakeries, if any, that sell Passover desserts and, if they do, they are usually not worth eating. The packaged Passover cakes and cookies often taste like cardboard. If you want flavorful Passover desserts, you have to bake them yourself. My goal here is to offer a range of great choices for every dessert category. In addition to the many gluten-free recipes in this chapter, you'll find nut-free, no-sugar-added, and vegan desserts, as well.

TRIPLE-CHOCOLATE BISCOTTI
{ gluten-free }

MAKES 24–36 COOKIES

PREP TIME 10 minutes

BAKE TIME 44 minutes

ADVANCE PREP May be made 5 days in advance or frozen

EQUIPMENT Measuring cups and spoons • Jelly roll pan or cookie sheet • Microwave-safe bowl or double boiler • Whisk • Silicone spatula • Knife • Cooling rack

These cookies are both chewy and crunchy at the same time; the outside is a little hard, but the center remains soft. I double this recipe because these cookies disappear so fast.

4 ounces (115g) bittersweet chocolate, broken into pieces

1 cup (200g) sugar

½ cup (120ml) vegetable oil

2 large eggs

3 tablespoons (40g) vanilla sugar (see box, page 98)

½ cup (40g) unsweetened cocoa

1 tablespoon potato starch

1½ cups (180g) ground almonds (see box, page 2)

¼ teaspoon salt

1 cup (170g) semi-sweet chocolate chips

PREHEAT oven to 350°F (180°C).

LINE a jelly roll pan or cookie sheet with parchment paper.

MELT the chocolate using one of the methods described in the box opposite. Remove the chocolate from the heat source, add the sugar and oil, and whisk well. Add the eggs and mix. Add the vanilla sugar, cocoa, potato starch, ground almonds, and salt and mix well. Add the chocolate chips and mix to distribute them.

DIVIDE the dough in half and shape into two loaves, each about 9 x 3 inches (23 x 7.5cm). Place both loaves on the lined jelly roll pan and bake for 30 minutes. Let the loaves cool for 10 minutes (do not turn off the oven). Cut each loaf crosswise into ¾- to 1-inch-thick (2- to 2.5-cm) slices. Place the cookies, cut side up, on a parchment-lined jelly roll pan. Bake for another 14 minutes, or until the cookies are firm to the touch on the outside but still feel soft on the inside. Check them after 10 to 12 minutes so that you don't overbake the cookies.

LET COOL for 5 minutes on the pan and then slide the parchment and cookies onto a cooling rack to cool completely.

MELTING CHOCOLATE

To melt chocolate, you can use the top part of a double boiler or a microwave oven. A double boiler is a specially designed saucepan that has a top bowl that fits snugly over a saucepan. For either method, first break or chop the chocolate into 1-inch (2.5-cm) pieces.

USING A DOUBLE BOILER: Place water in the bottom of the saucepan and place the chopped chocolate in the insert. When you bring the water to a simmer, it gently melts the chocolate in the insert. You can create your own double boiler by placing 2 to 3 inches (5 to 8cm) of water in a medium saucepan and resting a medium-size metal bowl containing the chopped chocolate on top. Stir the chocolate occasionally, until all of it has melted.

USING A MICROWAVE OVEN: Place the chocolate pieces in a microwave-safe bowl, such as a large glass bowl. Heat the chocolate for 1 minute at high power. Remove the bowl from the microwave oven and give the chocolate a good stir, mixing the melted pieces into the unmelted ones, for 30 seconds. Heat for another 45 seconds and stir well again. If the chocolate is not completely melted, heat it for another 30 seconds and stir. Repeat this process for another 15 seconds if necessary. Do not heat the chocolate in the microwave oven for several minutes straight or it will burn.

SHORTBREAD COOKIES
WITH ROYAL ICING
{ gluten-free }

**MAKES 20 (3-INCH/7.5-CM) MATZOH COOKIES
OR 48 SMALLER COOKIES**

PREP TIME 10 minutes; chill dough in the freezer
for 3 hours or overnight and then let dough thaw
for 10 minutes; 10 minutes to roll and cut dough;
15 minutes to chill cut cookies; 20 minutes for iced
cookies to dry

BAKE TIME 10–12 minutes per batch

ADVANCE PREP Dough may be made in advance
and frozen; cookies may be baked 3 days in
advance or frozen

EQUIPMENT Measuring cups and spoons • Food
processor • Rolling pin • Cookie sheets • Cookie
cutters or round drinking glass • Metal flat-blade
spatula • Cooling rack • Pastry bag and tips or a
small metal offset spatula to ice cookies

The success of this cookie was a surprise even to
me. I was working on the Pear Frangipane Tart
(on page 109) and had some dough left over. I
baked it and when I tasted it, I started jumping
up and down because it had the texture of
classic butter shortbread. Now you can make and
decorate sugar cookies for Passover, and your
gluten-free friends can eat them all year long. I
made the matzoh cookies pictured here using
royal icing as the base and then made the matzoh
lines with melted chocolate (from about ½ cup/
85g chocolate chips). Although they are pretty
when decorated, these cookies are just as tasty
without any adornment.

Tip: If you do not want to buy a rolling pin for use
during Passover, you can use a wine bottle.

FOR THE COOKIES

2½ cups (300g) ground almonds
  (see box, page 2)
1⅓ cups (160g) confectioners' sugar, plus
  more for dusting
1½ cups (240g) potato starch
½ cup (1 stick; 113g) margarine, frozen 30 minutes
  and then cut into pieces
2 tablespoons ice water
2 large egg yolks
½ teaspoon vanilla (optional) or scraped seeds
  of 1 vanilla bean (optional)

FOR THE ROYAL ICING

2 large egg whites
½ teaspoon vanilla (optional)
3¼ cups (390g) confectioners' sugar
About 2 tablespoons boiling water, or more
  as needed
Food coloring

To make the cookies

IN THE BOWL of a food processor fitted
with a metal blade, mix the ground almonds,
confectioners' sugar, and potato starch for 10
seconds. Add the margarine pieces and process
until the mixture resembles sand. Add the water,
egg yolks, and vanilla, if using, and process until
the dough comes together. Divide the dough in
half, wrap each piece loosely in plastic, and then
flatten the halves. Chill the dough in the freezer
for 3 hours or overnight.

PREHEAT oven to 400°F (200°C).

REMOVE the dough from the freezer and let
it thaw just until you can press into it gently.
Cut two pieces of parchment paper large
enough to line a cookie sheet and sprinkle a
little confectioners' sugar on one of the pieces;
place one of the discs of dough on top of the

PLACE the cookie sheets in the freezer for 15 minutes; this will help the cookies hold their shape while baking. Bake for 10 to 12 minutes, or until the cookies just begin to brown on the bottom; you should see very little color on the edges of the cookies. Check halfway through baking to see if the cookies on the back of the cookie sheet are browning faster than those on the front; if so, turn the cookie sheet around and continue baking. When the cookies are done, slide the parchment onto a cooling rack and let the cookies cool completely.

To make the icing

PLACE the egg whites and vanilla in a mixing bowl and beat with an electric mixer on medium-low speed until foamy, about 1 minute. Add the confectioners' sugar, 1 cup (120g) at a time, mixing on low speed and frequently scraping down the bowl with a silicone spatula. When all the sugar has been added, beat on high speed for 5 minutes, or until thick and shiny. Add teaspoons of boiling water one at a time, and mix until you achieve a consistency that you can spread. If the icing gets too loose, add some confectioners' sugar; if it's too thick, add more drops of boiling water.

DIVIDE the icing between bowls and color with food coloring as desired. You can use a small offset spatula to ice the cookies. For a more professional look, place the colored icings in pastry bags and use a small round tip. First ice a border on the cookies and then squeeze more icing into the center and spread to cover, either using the tip of the pastry bag or the offset spatula. Let dry at room temperature for 20 minutes.

paper, and then sprinkle the dough with a little confectioners' sugar. Place the second piece of parchment on top of the dough and use a rolling pin (or wine bottle) to roll out the dough until it is about ⅓ inch (8mm) thick. Every few rolls, peel back the parchment and sprinkle a little more confectioners' sugar on the dough. Remove the top piece of parchment paper and use it to line a cookie sheet. Line another cookie sheet with fresh parchment.

USE cookie cutters, a drinking glass, or a knife to cut out cookies and then use a metal flat-blade spatula to lift the cookies and place them on the prepared cookie sheets. Reroll any scraps and cut more cookies. If the dough becomes too soft, place it in the freezer until it gets firm. Repeat with the remaining piece of dough.

FULLY LOADED
COOKIE BARS
{ gluten-free }

**MAKES 24 (2-INCH/4.5-CM) SQUARE BARS
OR 49 (1 X 3-INCH/2.5 X 7.5-CM) BARS**
PREP TIME 15 minutes
BAKE TIME 30–35 minutes
ADVANCE PREP May be made 5 days in advance
or frozen
EQUIPMENT Measuring cups and spoons • Cutting
board • Knives • 9 x 13-inch (23 x 33-cm) baking
pan (for best results, don't use a disposable pan)
• Electric mixer or wooden spoon • Large mixing
bowl • Silicone spatula

I am declaring this the official snack bar of the
Passover holiday because these bars make
everyone happy. First, the ends are crunchy if
you like crisp cookies to dunk in milk, and the
middle is chewy if you like a gooey cookie. Next,
you can vary these cookie bars in so many ways.
Don't like coconut or raisins? Leave them out.
Love chocolate? Reduce the chopped nuts and
substitute some more chocolate chips. Start with
the base recipe the first time you make them and
then vary the add-ins as you like. In any case, you
will want to make these cookie bars more than
once over the holiday.

VANILLA SUGAR

If you cannot find vanilla sugar, you
can make your own by placing a whole
vanilla bean inside a container or jar with
2 cups of sugar. You can also use regular
sugar plus 1 teaspoon vanilla. (There is
no pure vanilla extract for Passover.)

1½ cups (300g) sugar
2 large eggs
1 cup (240ml) vegetable oil, plus extra for
greasing pan
2 tablespoons vanilla sugar (see box, below)
3¼ cups (390g) ground almonds (see box, page 2)
¼ cup (40g) potato starch
1 cup (180g) mini chocolate chips, or 1 bag
(10-ounce/280-g) chocolate chips
⅓ cup (40g) pecans, chopped into ½-inch
(12-mm) pieces
⅓ cup (40g) shelled pistachios, chopped into
½-inch (12-mm) pieces
⅓ cup (40g) walnuts, chopped into ½-inch
(12-mm) pieces
⅓ cup (30g) dried shredded coconut
⅓ cup (55g) golden raisins
⅓ cup (45g) dried cranberries

PREHEAT oven to 375°F (190°C).

GREASE a 9 x 13-inch (23 x 33-cm) baking pan
with oil and press in a piece of parchment paper
to cover the bottom and sides. Grease the top and
sides of the parchment.

IN A LARGE BOWL, beat the sugar, eggs, oil, and
vanilla sugar with an electric mixer on medium
speed, or mix well with a wooden spoon until
combined. Add the ground almonds and potato
starch and mix well. Add the chocolate chips,
pecans, pistachios, walnuts, coconut, raisins, and
cranberries and mix to distribute.

SCOOP the dough into the prepared pan and use
a spatula to spread it evenly. Bake for 30 to 35
minutes, or until the edges are brown and when
you insert a toothpick into the center, it has just a
few crumbs on it. Let cool. Lift out the parchment
and then cut into squares or bars.

ORANGE TEA CAKE CUPCAKES
{ gebrokts • nut-free }

MAKES 14 CUPCAKES
PREP TIME 10 minutes
BAKE TIME 25 minutes
ADVANCE PREP May be made 4 days in advance or frozen
EQUIPMENT Measuring cups and spoons • Zester • Electric mixer • Mixing bowl • Muffin tins and liners (can be disposable) • Medium bowl • Whisk • Silicone spatula • Small bowl

My Orange Tea Cake, flavored with orange and Earl Grey tea, graces the cover of my first book, *The Kosher Baker* (Brandeis, 2010), and it is one of my most popular recipes. I rarely go more than 3 weeks without baking it, so I decided that we all need a Passover version. These light, spongy cupcakes share the same flavor profile.

FOR THE CUPCAKES

⅓ cup (80ml) boiling water

1 Earl Grey or other black tea bag

1 cup sugar (200g), plus 1 teaspoon for the tea

4 large eggs, separated

1¼ teaspoons orange zest (from 1 orange), plus more for garnish, if desired

2 tablespoons fresh orange juice (from 1 zested orange)

⅓ cup (45g) matzoh cake meal

⅓ cup (55g) potato starch

Dash salt

FOR THE ICING

½ cup (60g) confectioners' sugar, plus more if needed

4 teaspoons reserved tea, plus more if needed

To make the cupcakes
PREHEAT oven to 375°F (190°C).

PLACE paper liners into 14 cups of two muffin tins.

MEASURE the boiling water into a bowl. Add the tea bag and 1 teaspoon sugar and let steep for 5 minutes. In a large bowl, with an electric mixer on low speed, beat the egg yolks, 3 tablespoons of the tea (reserve the rest), orange zest and juice, and sugar. Add the cake meal, potato starch, and salt and beat until combined.

IN A SEPARATE BOWL, beat the egg whites and salt on high speed until stiff peaks form. Using a silicone spatula, gently fold the whites into the bowl containing the egg yolk mixture, and then fill the muffin cups three-quarters full with the batter.

BAKE for 25 minutes, or until a toothpick inserted into the center of a cupcake comes out clean. Remove the cupcakes from the pan and let cool while you make the icing.

To make the icing
PLACE the confectioners' sugar in a small bowl. Add 4 teaspoons of the tea and whisk until you have a thick icing. Add more confectioners' sugar if the icing is too thin, more tea if it is too thick. To create a button or circle of icing on top of each cupcake, use a 1-teaspoon measuring spoon to scoop up icing and put it into the center of the cupcake, and then spread it slightly. Garnish with additional orange zest if desired.

EASY FRUIT CAKE
{ gluten-free }

SERVES 12–15
PREP TIME 10 minutes
BAKE TIME 45–50 minutes
ADVANCE PREP May be made 2 days in advance; cake is best reheated
EQUIPMENT Measuring cups and spoons • 9 x 13-inch (23 x 33-cm) baking pan • Medium bowl • Silicone spatula • Whisk

My friend Elena Lefkowitz is the master of taking a foolproof cake batter and turning it into a different cake every Shabbat, a talent that inspired this recipe. Passover bakers need a batter in their arsenal that they can mix and match with whatever fruit is on hand. This recipe will work with apples, pears, peaches, plums, and apricots, as well as any type of berry. Just make sure to measure 4 cups of fruit.

1 teaspoon oil for greasing pan
4 cups (700g) chopped fruit or mixed berries
1½ cups (180g) ground almonds (see box, page 2)
1 cup (200g) sugar
½ cup (80g) potato starch
5 large egg whites

PREHEAT oven to 400°F (200°C).

GREASE a 9 x 13-inch (23 x 33-cm) baking pan with oil and press in a piece of parchment to cover the bottom and sides. Scatter fruit on the bottom of the prepared pan.

PLACE the ground almonds in a medium bowl. Add the sugar, potato starch, and egg whites and whisk well.

SCOOP the batter over the layer of fruit as best you can (the batter will not cover all the fruit). Bake for 45 to 50 minutes, or until the top is browned. Serve warm or at room temperature.

OPERA CAKE
{ gluten-free }

SERVES 16
PREP TIME 25 minutes
BAKE TIME 15 minutes
ADVANCE PREP May be made 2 days in advance and stored in the fridge or frozen; coffee syrup may be made 5 days in advance
EQUIPMENT Measuring cups and spoons • Large mixing bowl • Whisk • 12 x 16-inch (30 x 40-cm) jelly roll pan • Electric mixer • 3 medium bowls • Silicone spatula • Metal offset spatula • Small saucepan • Cooling rack • Knives • Small cookie sheet • Microwave-safe bowl or double boiler • Pastry brush • Pastry bag and tip to decorate

This is a famous French chocolate and coffee dessert that you will see in the windows of every pastry shop in France and Switzerland. My favorite Opera Cake memory is from attending the bar mitzvah of the son of my friend Cathy Lawi, in Geneva. Movies were the theme of the bar mitzvah, and there was a huge cutout of the *Titanic* on one wall (with a Jewish star on it!). For dessert, a table was wheeled in with a 4-foot (1.25-m) replica of the *Titanic*, and on the decks were opera squares covered with sparklers. This dessert is usually made with French cooked butter cream and has four parts to it. I have spent years working on this recipe to streamline it and yet keep the tastes I love. This is a light hazelnut cake with deep coffee and chocolate flavors.

FOR THE GANACHE
1 pound (455g) bittersweet chocolate
1 cup (240ml) almond milk or whipping cream
3 tablespoons (45ml) strong brewed coffee or espresso

FOR THE HAZELNUT CAKE
6 large eggs, separated
3 tablespoons (40g) granulated sugar
1½ cups (180g) confectioners' sugar
1⅓ cups (150g) ground hazelnuts (see box, page 2)
⅔ cup (105g) potato starch
4 teaspoons vegetable oil

FOR THE COFFEE SYRUP
½ cup (100g) sugar
½ cup (120ml) water
2 tablespoons strong coffee or espresso

To make the ganache
MAKE the ganache first so that it firms up a bit while the cake is baking. Break the chocolate into small pieces and melt them either over a double boiler or in a microwave oven (see box, page 95 for both methods). Heat the almond milk until hot but not boiling. Add to the chocolate mixture a little at a time, whisking well after each addition. It will get very thick but will smooth out as you add more almond milk.

DIVIDE the ganache between two bowls, putting two-thirds into one bowl and one-third into the other. Cover and refrigerate the bowl containing one-third of the ganache. Into the second bowl, containing two-thirds of the ganache, add the coffee and whisk well. Cover and refrigerate for 15 to 20 minutes, or until the ganache thickens to a spreadable, not pourable, consistency. If the coffee-flavored ganache is not thick enough, when you are ready to assemble the cake, put the bowl in the freezer for 5 to 10 minutes and then whisk. If the ganache gets too hard, heat it in a microwave oven for a few seconds and whisk until smooth.

~ continued ~

To make the cake
PREHEAT oven to 375°F (190°C).

TRIM a piece of parchment paper to fit perfectly flat in the bottom of a 12 x 16-inch (30 x 40-cm) jelly roll pan.

IN A LARGE BOWL, use an electric mixer to beat the egg whites on high speed until stiff. Reduce the speed to low, add the granulated sugar, and beat for another 30 seconds. Transfer the beaten whites to a separate medium bowl. Into the bowl you just used to beat the whites, place the confectioners' sugar, ground hazelnuts, egg yolks, potato starch, and oil and beat for 1 minute on medium speed. (The mixture will be dry.) Add half of the beaten egg whites and mix well on medium speed for 30 seconds to combine. Scrape down the sides of the bowl with a silicone spatula. Use a whisk to mix in the remaining whites in two parts.

POUR the batter into the prepared pan. Use a metal offset spatula or silicone spatula to spread the batter as evenly as possible in the prepared pan. Bake for 15 minutes, or until lightly browned. Set aside to cool.

To make the coffee syrup
IN A SMALL SAUCEPAN, bring the sugar, water, and coffee to a boil and continue to boil for 3 minutes. Turn off the heat and let the syrup sit until ready for use. May be made up to 5 days in advance and stored, covered, at room temperature.

To assemble the cake
RUN a knife around the edges of the cake pan. Cover the pan with a piece of parchment paper and a cooling rack, and then flip the cake over onto the parchment and rack. Peel off the parchment on the bottom of the cake. Measure the midpoint on the long side of the cake and cut the cake in half to make two 6 x 8-inch (15 x 20-cm) rectangles. Place one half on a small cookie sheet lined with parchment, with the bottom of the cake facing up. Use a pastry brush to moisten every part of the cake with the coffee syrup.

USE a spatula to spread the chocolate ganache evenly on top of the cake all the way to the edges. Place the other cake half on top. Brush with syrup. Spread the coffee-flavored ganache on top, reserving about 2 tablespoons to decorate the cakes later, if desired. Heat a metal spatula under boiling water. Dry the spatula and then use it to smooth the top of the cake. Place the cake in the freezer until ready to serve. Put any extra ganache into a small bowl and refrigerate it until ready to decorate the slices.

To serve
TRIM ¼ inch (6mm) from all sides of the cake to even them out. Eat the trimmings. Heat a knife with hot water to cut the cake into rectangles. Clean and reheat the knife between slices to get perfect slices. Decorate the slices, if desired. Warm the reserved coffee ganache slightly to make it spreadable. Put it into a pastry bag with any shape tip you choose and pipe designs on top of each slice. You may add a coffee bean to the decor. If you do not have a pastry bag, to create some texture on the tops, heat the ganache to thin it, and then use a fork to drizzle chocolate lines or swirls over the slices. Store in the fridge.

GLAZED CHOCOLATE FUDGE SPONGE CAKE
{ gebrokts • nut-free }

SERVES 12

PREP TIME 20 minutes for cake; 5 minutes for glaze
BAKE TIME 50–60 minutes
ADVANCE PREP May be made 3 days in advance or frozen
EQUIPMENT 9- or 10-inch (23- or 25-cm) Bundt or tube pan (silicone is best) • Measuring cups and spoons • Cutting board • Knives • Electric mixer • Large mixing bowl • Microwave-safe bowl or double boiler • Whisk • Silicone spatula • Cooling rack and aluminum foil or waxed paper

In *The Holiday Kosher Baker*, I included a sponge cake recipe from my friend Annette Lerner that does not require separating eggs. The method is genius and truly results in a light sponge cake. Here is a chocolate version of that cake. Thanks to Dena Zack of Toledo, who came up with the idea for the glaze, which makes this cake even better, though the glaze is optional.

FOR THE CAKE
2 teaspoons oil plus 2 tablespoons potato starch or cake meal for dusting pan
11 ounces (310g) bittersweet chocolate, divided
9 large eggs
1½ cups (300g) sugar
¼ cup (60ml) vegetable oil
3 tablespoons (30g) potato starch
¼ cup (35g) matzoh cake meal
½ cup (40g) unsweetened cocoa
½ teaspoon salt

FOR THE GLAZE
4 ounces (115g) bittersweet chocolate
2 tablespoons margarine
⅓ cup (80ml) whipping cream

To make the cake
PREHEAT oven to 325°F (160°C).

GREASE a 9- to 10-inch (23- or 25-cm) Bundt or tube pan with 2 teaspoons oil and dust with 2 tablespoons potato starch or cake meal. Chop 6 ounces (170g) of the chocolate into ¼-inch (6-mm) pieces. Set aside.

IN A LARGE MIXING BOWL, with an electric mixer on high speed, beat the eggs and sugar for a full 5 minutes. Add the oil, potato starch, cake meal, cocoa, and salt and mix on low speed to incorporate. Increase the speed to medium and beat for another 5 minutes. Meanwhile, melt the remaining 5 ounces (140g) chocolate, either over a double boiler or in a microwave oven (see box, page 95), then add it to the batter and mix well. Add the chopped chocolate chunks and mix gently to distribute.

POUR the batter into the prepared tube pan. Bake for 50 to 60 minutes, or until a skewer inserted into the center comes out clean. Place a cooling rack on top of the cake and turn the pan with cake over onto the rack. Leave the pan on the cake and let cool. If you used a silicone pan, peel the pan off the cake; if you used an aluminum pan, turn it over, run a knife around the cake, and then turn it out. Let cool.

To make the glaze
MELT the chocolate and margarine, either over a double boiler or in the microwave (see box, page 95), and whisk well. Heat the whipping cream until hot and whisk into the chocolate. Place a large piece of aluminum foil under a cooling rack or place the cake directly on a piece of waxed paper. Use a silicone spatula to spread the glaze all over the cake until it is completely covered.

PISTACHIO AND STRAWBERRY ROLL
{ gluten-free }

SERVES 8–10

PREP TIME 20 minutes to chill strawberry puree; 3 hours to chill mousse; 5 minutes to prepare cake batter; 6 hours to freeze roll

BAKE TIME 15 minutes

ADVANCE PREP Mousse may be made 1 day in advance; filled roll may be frozen

EQUIPMENT Cutting board • Knives • Measuring cups and spoons • Food processor or blender • Silicone spatula • Whisk • Small saucepan • Sieve • Medium bowl • 12 x 16-inch jelly roll pan • Large bowl • Electric mixer • Cooling rack • Metal offset spatula • Cookie sheet • Clean dish towel

This is a cake that will impress everyone. It is beautiful, the flavors are subtle, and the dessert is light, making it perfect to serve after the long festive meal during the Seder. You can store the roll in the freezer, until people start clearing dinner plates, and then slice and plate it. By the time everyone is ready for dessert, the slices will have thawed enough to eat.

FOR THE STRAWBERRY MOUSSE

1 pound (455g) strawberries, trimmed
  and halved
Juice of 1 lemon
6 tablespoons (75g) granulated sugar
1 tablespoon plain unflavored kosher gelatin
  powder
½ cup (120ml) whipping cream

FOR THE PISTACHIO SPONGE CAKE

6 large eggs, separated
½ cup (100g) granulated sugar
1 teaspoon vanilla (optional)
⅓ cup (55g) potato starch
½ teaspoon fresh lemon juice
⅓ cup ground pistachio nuts, from about ¼ cup
  (30g) shelled nuts, (see box, page 2)
2 tablespoons confectioners' sugar

To make the mousse

PREPARE the mousse first to allow it time to chill. Place the strawberries in a blender or food processor fitted with a metal blade. Puree the strawberries completely, scraping down the sides of the bowl with a silicone spatula so that all the strawberry pieces are pureed.

PLACE the strawberry puree in a small saucepan and stir in the lemon juice and sugar. Cook on medium-low heat for 5 minutes, stirring occasionally, until the sugar melts. Whisk in the gelatin, and then remove the pan from the heat. Strain the strawberry mixture through a fine-mesh sieve into a medium bowl, pressing hard to get as much strawberry puree as possible through the sieve. Cover and place in the fridge for 20 minutes, whisking twice during that time.

WHIP the cream until stiff. Remove the strawberry puree from the fridge and fold in the whipped cream in four parts. Chill the mousse in the fridge for at least 3 hours or overnight.

To prepare the cake

PREHEAT oven to 375°F (190°C).

TRIM a piece of parchment paper to fit perfectly into the bottom of a 12 x 16-inch (30 x 40-cm)

~ continued ~

jelly roll pan. In a large bowl, whisk the egg yolks and granulated sugar until well combined. Add the vanilla, if using, and potato starch and whisk well.

PLACE the egg whites in the bowl of an electric mixer and beat on medium speed until foamy. Add lemon juice, increase the speed to high, and beat until stiff peaks form. Fold one-third of the whites into the egg yolk mixture and mix well. Add this mixture to the remaining whites and mix on low speed until combined. Add the ground pistachio nuts and mix in gently.

POUR the batter into the prepared jelly roll pan and use a silicone or metal offset spatula to spread evenly. Bake for 15 minutes, or until the top is lightly browned and the cake springs back when pressed gently. While the cake is baking, use a sieve to dust a clean dish towel with confectioners' sugar.

WHEN THE CAKE IS BAKED, remove it from the oven and immediately run a knife around the edges. Place a sheet of parchment paper over the cake, cover with a cooling rack, and flip the cake over onto the parchment paper. Peel off the parchment from the bottom of the cake. Lift the cake with the parchment paper underneath and turn the cake over onto the sugar-dusted towel. Remove the parchment. Lift up the towel under the cake on the short side of the cake and roll the cake up tightly with the towel inside. Make sure the seam of the cake roll is on the bottom when you are done rolling. Let cool for 20 minutes, or until cool to the touch.

To assemble the cake
WHEN YOU'RE READY TO ASSEMBLE THE CAKE, unroll the cake. Remove the mousse from the fridge and stir to soften. Use a silicone or offset

FRUIT SAUCES

Any plated dessert can be made even more beautiful when served with a fruit puree. You can serve the slice of cake in a pool of sauce, squeeze circles of sauce on the plate, or serve the sauce alongside.

STRAWBERRY, RASPBERRY, OR MANGO SAUCE

2 cups fruit
¼ cup hot water, or more as needed
2 teaspoons confectioners' sugar, or more to taste

PUREE together and strain if desired.

metal spatula to spread the mousse all over the cake to the edges. Starting from where you rolled before, roll up the cake with the mousse inside. With the seam on the bottom, lift the roll and place on top of a sheet of plastic wrap. Wrap tightly. Place on a cookie sheet and freeze for 6 hours or overnight.

To serve
REMOVE the roll from the freezer and cut a thin slice off both ends and eat them. Cut the roll into 1-inch (2.5-cm) slices and plate them. Allow the slices to thaw before serving, about 5 to 10 minutes.

PEAR FRANGIPANE TART
{ gluten-free }

SERVES 8–12

PREP TIME 40 minutes; chill dough for 3 hours; 25 minutes to poach pears

BAKE TIME 40–45 minutes to bake assembled tart

ADVANCE PREP Dough may be frozen; pears may be poached and almond cream may be made 3 days in advance; tart may be made 1 day in advance

EQUIPMENT Measuring cups and spoons • Cutting board • Knives • Food processor • Medium saucepan • Shallow bowl • Vegetable peeler • Small metal measuring spoon • Melon-baller • Slotted spoon • Electric mixer • Mixing bowl • Whisk • Silicone spatula • 8-inch (20-cm) tart or pie pan, or tart ring • Rolling pin (optional) • Cookie sheet • Metal flat-blade spatula • Sieve • Pastry brush

This classic French dessert has always been one of my most popular tarts. Do not worry about the multiple steps in this recipe: You can make the dough in advance (5 minutes) and freeze it, and make the almond cream (also 5 minutes) and poach the pears (30 minutes) 3 days before assembling and baking. I like to assemble and bake the tart the same day I serve it.

FOR THE TART CRUST

1¼ cups (150g) ground almonds (see box, page 2)

⅔ cup (80g) confectioners' sugar

¾ cup (120g) potato starch

4 tablespoons (57g) margarine, frozen 30 minutes and then cut into pieces

1 tablespoon cold water

1 large egg yolk

¼ teaspoon vanilla (optional)

FOR THE POACHED PEARS

6 cups (1.5L) water

1 cup (200g) granulated sugar

1 tablespoon vanilla, or substitute ½ cup (100g) vanilla sugar for half the regular granulated sugar (see box, page 98)

Juice of 1 lemon

3 firm Bosc or D'Anjou pears, about the same size and shape

FOR THE ALMOND CREAM

5 tablespoons (71g) margarine

⅓ cup (65g) granulated sugar

½ cup (60g) ground blanched almonds (see box, page 2)

1 tablespoon potato starch

1 large egg

2 teaspoons vanilla, or 1 tablespoon vanilla sugar

FOR THE FINISHED TART

2 tablespoons apricot jam

2 tablespoons confectioners' sugar, plus more for dusting

To make the crust

IN THE BOWL of a food processor fitted with a metal blade, place the ground almonds, confectioners' sugar, and potato starch and process for 10 seconds. Add the margarine pieces and process for another 10 seconds, or until the mixture resembles sand. Add the water, egg yolk, and vanilla and process just until the dough comes together. Gather into a ball, cover with plastic wrap, and flatten into a disc. Chill in the freezer for 3 hours or overnight.

To poach the pears

IN A MEDIUM SAUCEPAN, bring the water, sugar, and vanilla to a boil. Meanwhile, place the lemon juice in a shallow bowl. Slice off the very bottom

~ continued ~

and very top of each pear and peel them. Halve the pears from stem to bottom. With a small metal measuring spoon, starting at the top of one pear half, gently scoop out the thin vein that runs from the top to the bottom, the core, and the seeds. Try to retain the shape of the pear. Repeat with the remaining pear halves. Place pear halves into the lemon juice and turn to coat.

WHEN THE POACHING LIQUID has come to a boil, add the pears to the pot and simmer, uncovered, for approximately 25 minutes, or until the tip of a sharp knife slides easily into the inside of one of the pear halves; do not cut through.

LET THE PEARS cool in the saucepan and then transfer them to a bowl with one or two ladles of the poaching liquid. May be made 3 days in advance and chilled, covered, in the fridge.

To make the almond cream
WITH AN ELECTRIC MIXER or a whisk, beat the margarine on medium speed until soft. Add the sugar, ground almonds, and potato starch and beat again. Add the egg and vanilla. Increase the mixer speed to high and whip until the mixture is light and airy, about 1 minute. May be made 3 days in advance and stored, covered, in the refrigerator.

To prepare the tart
PREHEAT oven to 400°F (200°C).

PLACE the pear halves on paper towels to dry. Place an 8-inch (20-cm) tart pan, with or without a removable bottom, on a cookie sheet.

IF YOU DO NOT HAVE A ROLLING PIN, take pieces of dough, flatten them between your hands, and press them into the tart pan to cover the bottom and sides as evenly as you can. To use a rolling pin, sprinkle a piece of parchment paper with confectioners' sugar. Place the dough on top of the paper, sprinkle the dough with more confectioners' sugar, and cover with another piece of parchment paper. Roll the dough until it is an inch (2.5cm) larger than the pan. Remove the top parchment. Place your hand under the bottom parchment, lift the dough, and turn it over into the tart pan. Use your fingers to press the dough into the bottom and sides of the pan, patching up any holes with extra dough. Roll the rolling pin on top of the pan to trim off the excess dough. May be made several days in advance and stored in the freezer until ready to assemble the tart.

To assemble and bake the tart
USE a silicone spatula to spread the almond cream evenly on the bottom of the tart crust, all the way to the corners. Place each pear half on a small cutting board and use a small, sharp knife to cut crosswise into ¼-inch-thick (6-mm) slices (do not slice lengthwise from stem to base), being careful to retain the shape of the pear.

USE a metal flat-blade spatula to carefully pick up the entire sliced pear half (retain shape of the pear) and place on the cream, with the top of each pear facing toward the center. Repeat with the next pear half, placing it across from the first, the stem sides facing each other. Carefully place the remaining halves on the almond cream, spacing them evenly. With your finger, gently fan each pear from the center to the sides of the pan.

BAKE for 40 to 45 minutes, or until golden brown. Let cool.

To serve
WARM the apricot jam in the microwave for 15 seconds. Sift the confectioners' sugar over the baked almond cream and brush the pears with the jam. Store, covered, at room temperature.

FLOURLESS CHOCOLATE CAKE WITH MARSHMALLOW ICING
{ gluten-free • nut-free }

SERVES 12–16

PREP TIME 20 minutes; 4 hours to chill baked cake; 10 minutes to make icing

BAKE TIME 35 minutes

ADVANCE PREP May be made 3 days in advance or frozen

EQUIPMENT Cutting board • Knives • Measuring cups and spoons • 9- or 10-inch (23- or 25-cm) springform pan • Double boiler, heatproof bowl and medium saucepan, or microwave oven • Metal flat-blade spatula • Whisk • Hand-held electric mixer • Large mixing bowl • Silicone spatula • Blowtorch

Flourless chocolate cake is ubiquitous at Passover, but I began to tire of the same recipe year after year. Here, I've dressed up this classic dessert with a sweet cooked icing that perfectly complements the bitter chocolate cake.

FOR THE FLOURLESS CHOCOLATE CAKE
1 teaspoon oil for greasing pan
10 ounces (280g) bittersweet chocolate, roughly chopped
½ cup (1 stick; 113g) margarine
6 large eggs, separated, whites at room temperature (see box, facing page)
1 tablespoon unsweetened cocoa
½ cup (100g) sugar

FOR THE MARSHMALLOW ICING
1 cup (200g) sugar
¼ cup (60ml) warm water
2 large egg whites, at room temperature (see box, facing page)
1 tablespoon honey
Dash salt

PREHEAT oven to 350°F.

PLACE a piece of parchment on the counter and trace a circle around the bottom of a 9- or 10-inch (23- or 25-cm) springform pan. Cut out the circle.

GREASE the bottom of the pan with ½ teaspoon oil. Press the parchment circle on top. Grease the top of the parchment circle and the sides of the pan with the remaining oil. This step makes it easy to slide the finished cake onto a serving plate.

To make the cake
MELT the chocolate and margarine over a double boiler (see box, page 95), or use a heatproof bowl over a saucepan filled with simmering water, whisking often until thoroughly melted. You can also use a microwave oven, heating for 30-second

increments and mixing after each heating cycle until melted. When the chocolate and margarine are melted, remove from heat, add the egg yolks and cocoa, and whisk well.

IN A SEPARATE BOWL, with an electric mixer on high speed, beat the egg whites until stiff. Reduce the speed to low, add the sugar, a tablespoon at a time, and mix. When all the sugar has been added, turn the speed up to high for 1 minute.

FOLD the egg whites into the chocolate mixture in four parts, mixing more slowly after each addition. Pour the batter into the prepared pan.

BAKE for 35 minutes, or until the cake is set when jiggled. The cake will puff up and look cracked on top, but do not worry about that. Let cool, and the cake will fall a bit. Place in the fridge a minimum of 4 hours or overnight.

WHEN YOU'RE READY TO SERVE, open the spring and remove the sides of the pan. Use a metal flat-blade spatula to separate the parchment circle from the bottom of the pan and slide the parchment and cake onto a serving plate. You may tuck pieces of waxed paper or parchment paper under the cake to keep the platter clean when icing the cake.

To prepare the icing

POUR a few inches of water into the bottom of a double boiler or a medium saucepan and bring to a boil, then reduce the heat to medium. Off heat, place the sugar and warm water in the top of the double boiler, or in a heatproof bowl that can sit on top of the saucepan without falling in. Whisk to dissolve the sugar. Add the egg whites, honey, and salt and beat with a hand-held electric mixer for 1 minute on medium-high speed. Place the

bowl over the gently boiling water and beat with the hand-held electric mixer on high speed for a full 7 minutes. Remove from the heat.

TRIM any dry pieces from the top of the cake. Eat them. If the top of the cake is uneven, you may place a piece of parchment on top of the cake and turn it over to ice the bottom as the top. Use a metal spatula to spread the icing on the sides of the cake, and then scoop up and spread the icing onto the top of the cake to cover it. You can smooth the top and sides or, if you plan to toast them with a blowtorch, use a small spoon to create waves or texture on top. Remove the waxed paper or parchment pieces from under the cake. Store the cake in the fridge. Use the blowtorch to brown the waved edges until a golden-brown color is achieved.

BRINGING EGG WHITES TO ROOM TEMPERATURE IN 10 MINUTES

Separate the eggs and place the whites in a metal bowl. Place the bowl over another bowl filled with 2 inches (5cm) of hot water. Stir the eggs occasionally and they will be at room temperature within 10 minutes.

MERINGUE FRUIT TARTS
{ gluten-free • nut-free }

MAKES 10–12 TARTS

PREP TIME 20 minutes for meringue, 10 minutes to assemble

BAKE TIME 2 hours for shells, 30 minutes for lemon cream

ADVANCE PREP Meringue shells and lemon cream may be made 2 days in advance

EQUIPMENT Measuring cups and spoons • Cookie sheet or jelly roll pan • Zester • Cutting board • Knives • Electric mixer • Mixing bowl • Sieve • Double boiler, heatproof bowl over medium saucepan, or microwave oven • Whisk • Pastry bag • Large star pastry tip, such as Ateco #864 or #827

In this recipe, you bake meringue shells and fill them with lemon cream and fresh fruit. You can also fill the shells with whipped cream, chocolate mousse, ice cream, or sorbet.

FOR THE MERINGUE SHELLS

4 large egg whites, at room temperature for
  2 hours (or see page 113 to warm quickly)
2/3 cup (130g) granulated sugar
2/3 cup (80g) confectioners' sugar

FOR THE LEMON CREAM

2 large eggs plus 1 egg yolk
2/3 cup (130g) granulated sugar
Zest of 1/2 large lemon
4 tablespoons fresh lemon juice (from 2 lemons)
3 tablespoons (42g) margarine

FOR THE FINISHED TARTS

2 kiwis
1 cup berries
10 sliced strawberries and/or 1 mango, sliced

To make the meringue shells
PREHEAT oven to 220°F (105°C).

LINE a cookie sheet with parchment paper. Use a drinking glass to trace about a dozen 3-inch (7.5-cm) circles on the parchment paper and then turn the paper over on the cookie sheet.

IN A MIXING BOWL, with an electric mixer on high speed, beat the egg whites until stiff. Reduce the speed to low and add the granulated sugar, a tablespoon at a time, until incorporated. Return the speed to high and beat for a full 10 minutes, until thick and shiny. Sift the confectioners' sugar into the whites and mix in slowly.

FIT a pastry bag with a large star tip (1/2-inch/ 12-mm) opening. Spoon the meringue batter into the pastry bag. First squeeze out a circle just inside the drawn circles and then fill each circle with meringue batter to create a bottom. Next squeeze out a border on the edges of the circle. Repeat with a second layer on the borders so you have 10 or 12 meringue cups that are each 2 inches (5cm) high. Bake for 2 hours. Remove from the oven and let cool. Store in an airtight container at room temperature for up to 2 days.

To make the lemon cream
PLACE the eggs, yolk, sugar, lemon zest, and juice in a heatproof bowl and set over a medium saucepan with simmering water (or use a double boiler). Whisk well. Cook, uncovered, whisking occasionally, until a thick cream is formed. This takes approximately 30 minutes; be patient and do not stir too much. Add the margarine and whisk in. Chill until ready to use.

To assemble the meringue tarts
SCOOP 1 heaping tablespoon of lemon cream into each meringue shell and top with sliced fruit.

LINZER TART
{ gluten-free }

SERVES 8–12

PREP TIME 15 minutes; chill dough 45 minutes;
10 minutes to chill lattice strips

BAKE TIME 10–15 minutes for crust, 35–40 minutes
for tart

ADVANCE PREP May be made 4 days in advance
and stored covered at room temperature

EQUIPMENT Measuring cups and spoons • Large
bowl • Electric mixer • 8-inch (20-cm) round tart
pan (with or without a removable bottom) or pie
pan • Medium bowl • 2 cookie sheets • Silicone
spatula • Rolling pin • Knife or pastry wheel • Long
knife or metal spatula • Pastry brush to glaze top
of dough with egg white

This recipe may be the reason you buy a rolling
pin for Passover, which you can also use for the
shortbread cookies on page 96 or the pear tart
on page 109. In a pinch, a wine bottle works very
well. You can make this dessert with any flavor
jam you like. Sometimes I spread a red jam on
half the crust and apricot jam on the other half.
Here I use a pastry cutter, a small fluted wheel
on a handle, to cut the dough strips to achieve a
ridged look, but you can use a knife instead. The
crust requires 3 cups of three different kinds of
ground nuts; if you do not have enough of one
type, you can substitute another.

½ cup (1 stick; 113g) margarine
1½ cups (180g) ground almonds
1 cup (120g) ground walnuts
½ cup (55g) ground hazelnuts (with or
   without skins)
½ cup (80g) potato starch
¼ cup (50g) granulated sugar, plus 1½ teaspoons
   for sprinkling on top

½ cup (60g) confectioners' sugar, plus extra
   for dusting
1 cup (240ml) raspberry, apricot, or your
   favorite jam
1 large egg white, beaten, for glazing

To make the crust

IN A LARGE BOWL, with an electric mixer on high
speed, beat the margarine until soft, scraping
down the sides of the bowl with a silicone spatula
once or twice. Add the ground almonds, walnuts,
and hazelnuts along with the potato starch and
granulated sugar and mix. Separate a little more
than half the dough and put it into your tart or pie
pan. Leave the remaining dough in the bowl.

USE your hands to press the dough into the
bottom of the pan to cover it and create a
⅓-inch-thick (8-mm) crust on the sides. I find it
easiest to press the dough with my fingers into
the sides and corners of the pan first and then
with the palms of my hands press the dough into
the bottom of the pan to cover it with dough.
Take a little extra dough from the bowl if needed
to cover the bottom. Place the pan in the freezer.

ADD the confectioners' sugar to the smaller piece
of dough in the bowl and mix it in; the easiest
way is to use your hands. Shape the dough into
a ball and flatten it. Do not worry if the dough is
crumbly. Wrap the dough in plastic and place it in
the freezer for 45 minutes.

To make the tart

PREHEAT the oven to 375°F (190°C).

REMOVE the tart pan from the freezer and place
it on top of a cookie sheet. Bake for 10 to 15
minutes, or until the crust just starts to color.

REMOVE the pan from the oven, slide the parchment and tart pan off the cookie sheet, and let it cool for 5 minutes, or until the dough in the freezer is ready to be rolled out.

SPRINKLE a piece of parchment paper with some confectioners' sugar. Place the dough on top of the paper, sprinkle with more sugar, and cover it with another piece of parchment paper. With a rolling pin, roll the parchment-covered dough into a ⅓-inch-thick (8-mm) rectangle. Use a knife or pastry wheel to cut the dough into eight 1-inch (2.5-cm) strips. Slide the parchment onto a cookie sheet and freeze the strips for 10 minutes.

USE a silicone spatula to spread the jam evenly over the bottom of the crust.

REMOVE the dough strips from the freezer and use a long metal spatula or large knife to lift and place the strips across the top of the jam-filled crust to create a lattice. Do not try to bend the strips back to make a perfect over-and-under lattice. Instead, place half the strips in one direction, an inch apart, and then lay the others across them in the other direction. Trim the ends of the dough and press them into the border of the bottom crust. Brush the strips with the beaten egg white and sprinkle with the remaining 1½ teaspoons granulated sugar.

BAKE for 35 to 40 minutes, or until the jam is bubbling and the crust is golden brown. Serve warm or at room temperature.

CHEESECAKE WITH ROASTED CASHEW AND CHOCOLATE CRUST
{ dairy • gluten-free }

SERVES 16

PREP TIME 45 minutes for cream cheese to soften; 20 minutes to prepare; 15 minutes to chill crust; 10 minutes to make the brittle; 5 hours to chill cake

BAKE TIME 1 hour and 10 minutes, plus 1 hour to cool in oven

ADVANCE PREP May be made 4 days in advance or frozen; brittle may be made 3 days in advance

EQUIPMENT Cutting board • Knives • Measuring cups and spoon • Wooden spoon • Jelly roll pan • Zester • Electric mixer • Large mixing bowl • Microwave-safe bowl or double boiler • 9- or 10-inch (23- or 25-cm) springform pan • Silicone spatula • Whisk • Cookie sheet • Small heavy saucepan • Pastry bag and tip for piping whipped cream (optional)

I came to appreciate cheesecake on Passover during a trip to Israel, where every hotel breakfast buffet offered several cheesecake options, many served like a baked pudding that you eat with a spoon. Israeli cheesecakes are lighter than the dense American ones, which are made almost entirely of cream cheese, because in Israel they use a lighter cheese called *gevina levana* that results in a light, airy, but still creamy texture. I added cream to this cheesecake batter to achieve a lighter cake, more like the Israeli version. It does not slice as perfectly as the all-cream cheese version, but do not let that deter you from trying this creamy, tasty cake.

FOR THE CRUST

1 cup (120g) raw unsalted cashews

8 ounces (225g) bittersweet chocolate

2/3 cup (160ml) milk or whipping cream

2 tablespoons unsalted butter, at room
temperature, plus 1 tablespoon for greasing pan

1/2 teaspoon ground cinnamon

1 teaspoon orange zest (from 1 large orange)

FOR THE FILLING

1 1/2 pounds (675g) cream cheese (not whipped),
at room temperature for at least 45 minutes

1/2 cup (120ml) heavy cream

4 large eggs

1 cup (200g) sugar

1 teaspoon orange zest (from the same orange
used for the crust)

FOR THE CASHEW BRITTLE

1/3 cup (65g) sugar

2 tablespoons water

1/2 cup (60g) raw unsalted cashews

Dash salt

FOR THE TOPPING

1/2 cup (120ml) whipping cream

To make the crust

PREHEAT oven to 325°F (160°C).

PLACE the cashews on a jelly roll pan and roast
for 15 to 20 minutes, until brown and fragrant. Let
cool and then chop roughly into 1/3-inch (8-mm)
pieces.

YOU WILL NEED a 9- or 10-inch (23- or 25-cm)
springform pan. Trace the bottom of the pan
on parchment paper and cut out the circle. Using
1 tablespoon of butter, rub around the bottom and
sides of the pan. Press the parchment circle into

the bottom of the pan and grease the top of the
parchment.

BREAK the chocolate into small pieces and melt
over a double boiler or in the microwave oven
(see box, page 95). Heat the milk or cream and
whisk, in four parts, into the chocolate. Add the
butter, cinnamon, and orange zest and whisk well.
Add the toasted nuts and mix well. Scoop the
mixture into the prepared pan and use a silicone
spatula to spread it on the bottom of the pan.
Freeze for 15 minutes to firm up.

To make the filling

IN A LARGE MIXING BOWL, with an electric mixer
on medium-high speed, beat the cream cheese
until smooth, scraping down the sides of the bowl
with a silicone spatula several times. Add the
whipping cream and beat until smooth. Add the
eggs, one at a time, scraping down the bowl after
each addition to make sure all the cream cheese
and eggs are being mixed together. Add the sugar
and orange zest and mix on medium speed until
combined. Make sure to scrape the bottom of the
bowl to ensure that the mixture is entirely smooth.
Scrape off any pieces of zest stuck on the beaters
and mix into the batter.

POUR the cheesecake batter on top of the crust.
Bake for 1 hour and 10 minutes. Turn off the oven
and prop the oven door open with a wooden
spoon. Leave the cake in the oven (to firm up)
for another hour. Let cool on a wire rack until the
cake is completely cooled. Chill in the fridge for 5
hours or overnight.

To make the brittle

LINE a cookie sheet with parchment paper or a
nonstick silicone mat. In a small heavy saucepan
over medium-high heat, heat the sugar and water

~ continued ~

without stirring until the mixture starts to color around the edges, about 5 minutes. Add the cashews and salt and then stir with a wooden spoon. Reduce the heat to medium-low and continue cooking. The mixture will get dry, but then the sugar will melt and the mixture will turn golden. Stir often and be patient. When the nuts are toasted and surrounded by a medium-colored caramel, pour onto the prepared pan and spread out as much as possible. Let cool. May be made 3 days in advance and stored in a resealable plastic bag or container at room temperature.

To serve

WHIP the cream until stiff. Either use a spatula to spread a thin layer over the top of the cake, or place whipped cream into a pastry bag fitted with a large round or star tip and pipe dots, lines, or stars on top of the cake. Break the brittle into pieces and decorate as desired.

DATE AND PISTACHIO ROLL
{ gluten-free • no added sugar • vegan }

MAKES 16 SLICES
PREP TIME 10 minutes; chill for 3 hours
ADVANCE PREP Store in the fridge for up to 1 week
EQUIPMENT Food processor • Large bowl • Measuring cups and spoons • Cutting board • Knives • Electric mixer and bowl (optional)

In 2013, my oldest children, Emily and Sam, were both on programs in Israel for the semester, so the rest of us went to visit them. We arrived in Jerusalem the weekend before Passover, and my goal was to eat as much bread and as many pastries as possible before the holiday. The day before Passover we went to the Machane Yehuda market, which is basically heaven for foodies like me. I tasted as much as I could, especially food I would not be able to eat during Passover. There were so many stalls with Passover cookies and candies, too. Among them I found a stack of dried fruit and nut rolls and thought they would make a super-easy Passover candy—with no added sugar.

15 ounces (430g) dates (Medjool are best), pitted
½ teaspoon vanilla (optional)
¼ teaspoon ground cinnamon
⅔ cup (130g) dried apricots (5 ounces/140g), chopped into ½-inch (12-mm) pieces
1 cup (120g) shelled pistachio nuts
½ cup (75g) whole almonds

PLACE the dates into the bowl of a food processor fitted with a metal blade. Add the vanilla, if using, and cinnamon and process until the dates form a smooth paste and the mixture comes together into a ball. Transfer the paste to a mixing bowl and either use your hands or an electric mixer to knead in the apricot pieces, pistachios, and almonds.

CUT OFF a 20-inch-long (50-cm) piece of parchment paper. Place the date mixture on the parchment and shape it into a 9- to 10-inch-long (23- to 25-cm) log that is 2½ inches (6-cm) thick, like a salami. Wrap the log tightly in the parchment paper and squeeze tightly. Unroll the log and then roll it up two more times on the counter, squeezing while rolling. Twist both ends of the parchment to seal the roll. Place it in the fridge for 3 hours to firm up. To serve, slice into ½- or ¾-inch-thick (12-mm- or 2-cm) slices.

TORRONÉ CANDY
{ gluten-free }

SERVES 12
PREP TIME 20 minutes
BAKE TIME 8 minutes
ADVANCE PREP May be made 1 week in advance
EQUIPMENT Cutting board • Knives • Measuring cups • 8-inch (20-cm) square baking pan • Small saucepan • Candy thermometer • Electric mixer • Mixing bowl • Silicone spatula

This is a chewy candy that is popular in both Italy and Provence. In Italy, it is called Torroné (pronounced "*toronay*") and in France it is called Nougat de Montélimar, the town where the candy originated. It has a long shelf life, so if you cut off small pieces and tightly cover the candy in plastic, you can enjoy it all holiday long.

½ cup (75g) whole almonds
1 cup (120g) shelled pistachios
⅔ cup (90g) dried cranberries
Oil for greasing pan
1 large egg white, at room temperature
   (see box, page 113)
1 cup (200g) sugar
½ cup (120ml) honey
Dash salt

ROUGHLY CHOP the almonds, pistachios, and cranberries into ⅓-inch (8-mm) pieces and set aside.

GREASE an 8-inch (20-cm) square baking pan with oil and line with parchment. Generously grease the top of the parchment with more oil. Set aside. Place the egg white into a mixing bowl. Set aside.

IN A SMALL SAUCEPAN, heat the sugar and honey over medium heat and stir until sugar is melted. When the thermometer reads 240°F (115°C), use an electric mixer to start beating the egg white and salt until soft peaks form. When the temperature reaches 260°F (125°C), reduce the mixer speed to low and slowly pour the sugar and honey syrup down the side of the bowl. When it is all poured in, increase the mixer speed to high and beat for 10 minutes.

ADD the reserved almonds, pistachios, and cranberries and use a silicone spatula to distribute. Scoop the candy mixture into the prepared pan. Spray or rub the top with oil and press a piece of waxed paper on top. Let cool to room temperature. May be stored, wrapped in plastic, for up to 1 week. Cut into small pieces to serve.

ABOUT THE AUTHOR

PAULA SHOYER is the author of *The Kosher Baker: Over 160 Dairy-free Recipes from Traditional to Trendy* (Brandeis 2010) and *The Holiday Kosher Baker: Traditional & Contemporary Holiday Desserts* (Sterling 2013). A former practicing attorney, Paula graduated from the Ritz Escoffier pastry program in Paris in 1996 and teaches cooking and baking classes in French pastry and Jewish cooking in the Washington, DC, area and does demonstrations all around the world. She serves as a consultant to several kosher bakeries. TV appearances include Food Network's *Sweet Genius*, WGN's *Lunchbreak*, *Daytime*, news shows *WUSA9 Washington, San Diego Living, NBC Washington and Baltimore,* and *Kojo Nnamdi Show* and *Martha Stewart Living* radio shows. Paula develops dessert recipes that are dairy-free, sugar-free, gluten-free, and vegan. She is a freelance writer for the *Washington Post, Kosher Scoop*, and *Jewish Food Experience* websites, and *Whisk, Joy of Kosher*, and *Hadassah* magazines. Paula lives in Chevy Chase, Maryland, with her husband and four children. You can find Paula at *www.thekosherbaker.com and information about how to bring her to your community*.

ACKNOWLEDGMENTS

FIRST, thank you to the greatest husband and children one could ever ask for. Andy, Emily, Sam, Jake, and Joey: all of you believed that, of course, I could write an entire book in just a few months. Thank you for enduring five full months of Passover and tasting these recipes over and over again. I love you all.

Thank you to my parents, Toby and Reubin Marcus, and mother-in-law, Lillian Shoyer, who give me love and support, but secretly believe I must be out of my mind to work so hard on a new book during a book tour. Arthur Shoyer, may his memory be a blessing, would not have doubted me for a second.

Thanks to my brothers, Ezra and Adam Marcus, who know firsthand the Passover experiences that shaped this book.

I am indebted to my fabulous team of recipe-testers who make sure all the recipes in this book work in homes other than mine. Thanks to Rhonda Alexander-Abt, Elena Lefkowitz, Marla Satinsky, Mark and Melissa Arking, Esther Dayon, Trudy Jacobson, Suzi Brozman, Sylvia Blickstein, Sue Stein, Dena Zack, Bonnie Berland, Katie Wexler, and Andrea Neusner. Thanks to my other cheerleaders: Debby Horowitz, Tamar Dascal, Suzin Glickman, Judith Gold, Amanda Goldstein, Lily Starr, Laurie Strongin, and Karina Schumer. Special gratitude to the talented cook and entertainer Limor Decter, who serves as general consultant and kosher food maven for every one of my books.

I have been blessed with an amazing assistant, Diana Ash, without whom I could never have produced a book of this quality in a short time frame. Diana tested and retested all these recipes until we achieved great results and helped cook and bake for the photo shoot. You are a great tester, editor, and troubleshooter, as well as a very talented food stylist.

Once again I am humbled by the fabulous work of photographer Michael Bennett Kress. Thanks to Lisa Cherkasky, who styled the savory food photos. A second thanks to florist Marla Satinsky for the floral arrangements.

Thank you to Lily Starr, Kathy Ingber, and Dana Marlowe for generously lending me some of the beautiful dishes and objects featured on these pages. Thanks to Deb Shalom of Leila Jewels in Potomac, Maryland, for lending me the gorgeous Seder plate by artist Melanie Dankowicz, featured on page xiv. Appreciation for the talent of Ivy Dashti of Ra'anana, Israel, for the ceramic Seder plate on the cover.

More thanks to my brother Adam Marcus, a great editor, who found time to edit even while our father was in and out of the hospital.

Special thanks to Sally and Lisa Ekus who continue help me achieve my professional goals.

Thanks to Sterling editor Jennifer Williams, who brought me this project a mere *two* weeks after *The Holiday Kosher Baker* was released. How's that for support from a publisher? Special thanks to book designer Elizabeth Mihaltse, who came to DC to help style the breakfast, dessert, and cover shots. More thanks to the team at Sterling: Theresa Thompson, Trudi Bartow, Marilyn Kretzer, Rodman Neumann, Sue Levitt, Hannah Reich, Chris Thompson, Christine Heun, Merideth Harte, Ellen Day Hudson, and Gretl Rasmussen, as well as Joyce Cohen, Sarah Scheffel, Barbara Balch, Kristin Vorce, and Jay Kreider.

BIBLIOGRAPHY

The Family Haggadah (ArtScroll Mesorah 2009)

A Passover Haggadah, Elie Wiesel (Touchstone 1993)

Leading the Passover Journey, Rabbi Nathan Laufer (Jewish Lights Publishing 2005)

Encyclopedia of Jewish Food, Gil Marks (Wiley 2010)

INDEX

Note: Page numbers in *italics* indicate photographs on pages separate from recipes.

(continued)